Cre

Cha

MW01490655

Highlights & Commentary on Henry Morris,
Michael Behe, Stephen Meyer, Jonathan Wells,
& Others

Nate Richardson

This edition was updated 11.29.24. Copyright Nate Richardson 2024. This book may be shared for non-profit purposes. Visit RichardsonStudies.com for similar resources.

Nate Richardson is the editor of RichardsonStudies.com, a faith-based research organization. Nate is a member of The Church of Jesus Christ of Latter-day Saints. If you would like to contribute or discuss material, contact Nate at editor@richardsonstudies.com.

Contents

In this book I highlight the works of a cloud of witnesses in the creation science realm.

These notes highlight a few key ideas in my own words, be sure to refer to these master works to dive much deeper into these topics.

When inserting ideas of my own, I indicate such by "Note - …"

Review of Universal Model: A New Millennial Science Textbooks Vols. 1 & 2 by Dean Sessions

I've never seen a science work, even a creation science work, make religion so obviously scientific. It makes a strong case for religion as a reasonable central thing which goes with science.

The strength of UM is that it demonstrates the 7000 year creation as set forth in scripture, and shows my citing many academics and conducting experiments, that these doctrines are what science naturally demonstrates.

Ch. 1-4 Introduction: This gets people ready to understand that modern science is WAY off. People might see the "big pic of modern science" (against Darwin and Einstein) at first without seeing the evidence and automatically reject UM (of course it's inherently hard sharing new ideas with the world and we can't get everyone on board).

Ch. 5 Magma – In the Ch. 7 on water we see lots of answers which the magma chapter poses. The diagrams and images were extra helpful to clearly dismantle the magma theory.

Ch. 6 Rocks –These are writings preparatory for the flood chapter and require an understanding of the magma pseudo-theory.

Ch. 7 Hydroplanet – Revolutionary findings to finally prove the old water-planet idea held by people long ago. Here the magma mysteries are answered.

Ch. 8 Universal Flood – This chapter answers mysteries posed in the rock chapter. Hundreds of geological evidences are given for the worldwide flood.

Ch. 9 Weather – Helps clear up confusing meteorology. There were exciting concepts here, the geofield, very exciting.

Ch. 10 Age – Throws down hard on radiometric dating, lots of great examples, enjoyed the DNA and dendrochronology etc., the true dating as well as the exposing false. I like the 1 day to 1000 years conversion from scripture being applied to scientific research.

This chapter will open people's eyes to how shaky modern science is since the age of earth is so dogmatically promoted.

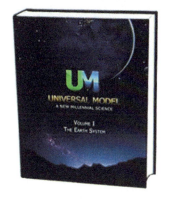

The Earth's core is important for knowing the Earth's age once one puts the pieces together.

Ch. 11 Fossils – Most are surprised to hear of the flood fossilizing everything, UM nailed how it happened by successful experimentation. All of UM is anti-evolution, just taking on different aspects of that battle.

Ch. 12 Evolution – It's nice that UM includes a few overviews of some contributions from other creation science texts in here too. UM gives credit where it's due and takes things to a whole new level. The magma exposé brings a whole new branch of strength to the anti-evolution topic which most people miss.

Here are some great illustrations and a few scientists quoted from the evolution chapter of UM, as well as related chapters (actually the whole of the UM books are all against evolution):

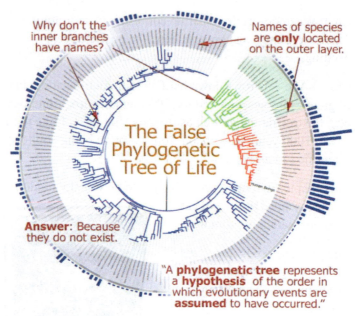

(Image: Universal Model 2)

(Image: Universal Model 2)

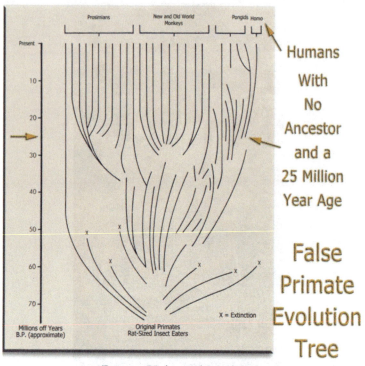

Prosimians

New and Old World Monkeys

Pongids Homo

Humans With No Ancestor and a 25 Million Year Age

Present

10

20

30

40

50

60

70

X = Extinction

Millions off Years B.P. (approximate)

Original Primates Rat-Sized Insect Eaters

False Primate Evolution Tree

(Image: Universal Model 2)

Soil Formation Evidence

Only one layer of organic soil on surfaces worldwide.
No multiple layers created over 'millions' of years.
Quantitative measurements indicate the soil formed ~4,000 years ago.
Does this look like Universal Flood evidence to you?

The above image from Universal Model Vol. 1 Ch. 8 demonstrates that continents weren't subducted and uplifted multiple time as modern geology claims, and that thickness of the organic soil layer on the surface indicates the time each layer took to form. Because soil formation times can be generally determined, these soil layers indicate a worldwide event took place only several thousand years ago, depositing the sediment beneath the topsoil layer.

"One of the major stumbling blocks is the **lack of evidence** concerning fossil forms and the **ignorance about the direction of evolutionary trends and rates** of evolution. This creates a serious problem, since **without data, weighting of characters in classification is <u>largely subjective, and a truly evolutionary classification will never be a reality</u>**." Frank E. Poirier, Fossil Evidence, p12; Universal Model 2 p180

"We have a desire to see the story of **bipedalism as a linear**, **progressive** thing… but **evolution doesn't evolve toward anything**; it's a **messy** affair, full of diversity and dead ends." (Will Harcourt-Smith – Anthropologist, American Museum of Natural History)

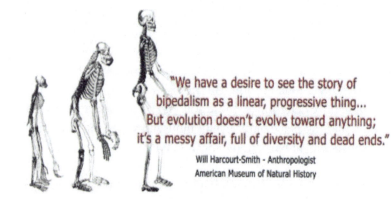

"We have a desire to see the story of bipedalism as a linear, progressive thing... But evolution doesn't evolve toward anything; it's a messy affair, full of diversity and dead ends."

Will Harcourt-Smith - Anthropologist
American Museum of Natural History

"…the human family of species are arranged in an orderly procession from **primitive forms up to modern Man**. But such scenarios are **subjective**…they are **unscientific**." (Henry Gee)

(Images from Universal Model 2)

Radiocarbon Dated Living Rats:
-260 to 2,139 Years Old

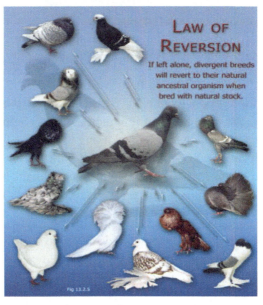

LAW OF
REVERSION

If left alone, divergent breeds
will revert to their natural
ancestral organism when
bred with natural stock.

Fig 13.2.5

"No one has actually witnessed
the birth of a species in the wild..."
Science, 25 June 1999, p2106

Ch. 13 Living – Makes clear laws of living things, exciting to start seeing the higher intelligence be emphasized. The earth as a pond idea was awesome. The microbe stuff is certainly revolutionary and makes God obvious.

Ch. 14 History – Fascinating language record based on the tower of Babel. The simplicity of the 3 original races was mind-blowing. The family history chart of someone back to Adam was very exciting.

Both history and science are fraught with error, and UM is an epic help to be grounded as we approach those subjects, a reminder to take the Bible seriously and literally, etc.

Ch. 15 Clovis – Human fossil artifacts in the USA show the pre-flood people lived there. This I'm sure will be news to many. We have a hint of it in the Latter-day Saint religion; this sets the stage for demonstrating the Book of Mormon as a historical text (Adena Jaredites, Hopewell Nephites, etc.). All of this helps prove that God placed humans here at a certain time, that humans haven't lived on earth for so long.

Ch. 16 Human – I loved the stuff throwing down against childlessness and abortion. Kids these days want to know why having children is important, this shows why in a way important even for those who don't believe in God.

Some kids reject God and everything to do with God when they don't like a particular church. UM helps show how God is reasonable, and how basic concepts of faith are important even for those who don't have a religion they trust yet. It helps them not be atheist, however popular. It demonstrates that religious people are happier, etc. There were good demonstrations in psychology and successful family life in this chapter.

I loved the political science model and the boldness in showing that we need a balance and a medium, but also showing that the liberals have taken over and are toxic. UM does that in a scientific way. I love it when UM is bold! Truth has permission to be bold!

In the medical model I found lots of new ideas which renewed my faith not only in good nutrition, but in herbalism and natural methods to help irregular conditions improve. The Jethro Kloss Back to Eden stuff about natural medicine is fascinating. I know his ideas need to be proven like any other idea, but I do see the weight of evidence from his healing many people. Naturally, the academic journals etc. will do everything they can to get rid of these things which don't cost boatloads of money, and which cure people (getting rid of their return clients)!

UM exposes many conspiracies. The Book of Mormon certainly warns us to beware these secret combinations. The conspiracies often go deeper than most are willing to admit. UM does well with the vaccine writings, showing they have potential, but are typically useless and dangerous.

This subchapter advocates natural whole foods, and advocates eating plant based.

UM shows that the human was meant for life on earth, that such proves a creator, that we don't thrive in artificial environments, and that this applies to what we eat as well. Brilliant. It proves life is intentional and full of purpose.

The noetic science stuff was interesting. UM makes a great point that conscience is beyond science, that we can prove that the spiritual realm is real, etc. UM endorses the idea that people (like prophets and other inspired individuals) can have information in ways which are purely spiritual. We say faith is just for religion, but UM shows it's for science. We also say religion is just faith, but perhaps someday soon people will recognize much of religion is provable, and UM has done well at highlighting this.

UM mentions that the psychics who didn't charge for their services were typically the most successful, that would make sense.

UM highlights that scientists are openly anti-religion. It does a great job at proving this, and it helps paint the picture overall that history, including the Bible, is fundamental to science. It shows that Godless science doesn't work!

The human model covers topics more people are familiar with and will be quite easy reading for the public. All of UM is understandable, but this chapter people already know something about, and they'll have quite an easy time with.

Volume 2 introduces the social sciences, not just the hard sciences into the picture, and it makes UM all the more beautiful and simple, not being afraid of these controversial subjects, these more 'subjective' sciences; UM makes them more objective, and shows how bias and atheistic agendas have made social sciences into watered down and less useful, and by doing this UM shows how correct use of social sciences can be very useful. Everyone would do well to remember that we have potential for both physical and social science in a good way.

Darwin's Doubt by Stephen Meyer – Book Highlights & Commentary

This was written
after his landmark
"Signature in the
Cell" book. He
responds to some
criticism of his
work there.
This is an excellent

and detailed book going over specific evolutionist claims.
My notes here only reflect a few general principles.

Here is a summary of the book which he gives toward the
end. 4 specific scientific critiques of the inadequacy of
Neo-Darwinism in this book are
"1. Neo-Darwinism has no means of efficiently searching
available combination space for functional genes and
proteins and consequently
2. It requires unrealistic unrealistically long waiting times
to generate even a single new Gene or protein, and the new
mechanism cannot produce body plans because
3. Early acting mutations, the only kind capable of
generating large-scale changes, are also invariably
deleterious and
4. Genetic mutations cannot in any case generate the
epigenetic information necessary to build a body plan."

Darwin saw the lack of transitional fossils as the one big
problem in his theory. He hoped later researchers would
find them, but no one has. Dogmatic Darwinists are more
confident about the theory than Darwin himself was.

Darwin was at least able to confess the weakness of his theory when it came to the lack of transitional fossils.

One Chinese scientist pointed out that in China you can't question the government, but you can question Darwin; in America you can question the government, but you can't question Darwin!

Scientific literature in every field is raising serious problems with Neo-Darwinism.

Darwin was all about a universal common ancestor, and natural selection being how we have variety today.

Evolutionists say the soft and hard parts of animals had to evolve at the same time since the animal couldn't survive with just the soft part.

There are many fossils of soft parts of animals which goes against Darwin's longtime theory.

Many fossils are even more complex than the animals of today, which goes against Darwin's simple to complex theory.

There are Precambrian fossils of tiny soft animals, but not of transitional fossils; if even the tiny soft animals were preserved then necessarily the other transitional animals would have been too. Lots of data indicates that transitional animals never existed, and this is true even though many pre-Cambrian environments were ideal for fossilization.

With how much we know about the fossil record now we can't claim that these transitional fossils might be out there somewhere. It's like reaching into a bag of marbles and pulling out blue, red and yellow. At first you think the whole rainbow might be in there, but as you keep pulling out marbles and you only get the same three colors, so you can't keep saying that it's likely that the whole rainbow is in there, much less the whole spectrum of colors between each color.

Scientists now see the Cambrian explosion happened in a much shorter duration of time than previously thought.

They say the Cambrian explosion is like one minute of a 24-hour day when compared to the age of Earth. Evolutionists play word games to try and make it seem like they came in an explosion which took many millions of years, claiming a series of explosions etc. Evolutionists are always 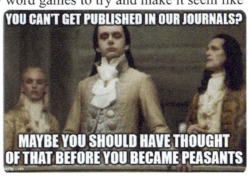 trying to find ways to make the Cambrian explosion appear less explosive.

Meyer does lots of debates and discusses some of those in the text. *(Note – he is one of the greatest debaters.)*

Many fossils which aren't even animals are claimed to be intermediate animal fossils.

There are many leaps in complexity in a relatively short geologic time, which natural selection cannot account for. They have been called 'quantum leaps.'

Neo-Darwinism is like classical Darwinism, requiring significant amounts of time, and Neo-Darwinism focuses on mutations. They claim that in the Cambrian and Ediacaran periods that significant mutations took place over 40 million years, which is not nearly enough for natural selection to make those changes. That's why they call these 'explosions.'

The first principle is do not fool yourself, you are the easiest person to fool. If you fool yourself, you'll fool others.

They come up with names for intermediate branches on their phylogenic tree when no discoveries of those animals have been made, it's just a name a placeholder!

Scientists will admit amongst themselves weak points of their theories, but in public they deny or undermine those points.

Homologous structures were known to be signs of a common designer until evolutionary theorists foisted their dogmatic view on everyone, insisting that these rather mean a common ancestor.

Evolutionists downplay the Cambrian explosion claiming that millions of years of evolution caused that explosion, but that this evolution was all hidden!

Scientists admit that there is overwhelming evidence in the fossil record that animals evolved long before evolution theory claims they would have.

Note - this does not refer to deep time, this refers to the order that fossils are found.

Scientists admit that whenever you see a time in geologic literature, you should demand uncertainty.

Scientists claim that we already know that life evolved from a common ancestor, so they automatically reject findings which don't agree with that conclusion.

Scientists admit there is no tree of phylogenic life pointing to a common ancestor. Genes do not give information about evolutionary relationships.

Molecular and anatomical data frequently disagree, leaving scientists arguing about how to classify them.

We know of many cases when similarity does not indicate common ancestry. Evolutionists repeatedly invoke convergent evolution to uphold their theory from collapse, while convergent evolution goes against all of their homology arguments. The whole phylogenic tree is based on similarity being a reliable indicator of ancestry, and as we see they don't have this anymore.

There's no consistent coherent way to organize all animals into a family tree.

Imagine that you're invited to a reunion of distant family. You get there and you're supposed to organize yourselves into first cousins, second cousins, etc. based on appearance and common ancestry stories. But the more you talk to the people at the event, the more you realize you don't have the same story and not many people there look like you at all. This is what we have with the animal classification and the phylogenic tree of life. (The analogy breaks down when you consider that all humans were from a common human ancestor, but all living things were not.)

Punctuated equilibrium theory is a way to try to confront the stasis in the fossil record, in other words the lack of transitional fossils which Darwin's gradualistic theory requires. Punctuated equilibrium is about long periods of nothing happening and then lots of things happening and then back to long periods of nothing. (The only reason they have long periods of nothing is to account for traditional evolution time.) Gould was very popular for advocating this.

Meyer debunks allopatric speciation and punctuated equilibrium. These theories require unusual speed and flexibility.

Mendel showed that Darwin's idea of blended inheritance is not correct. The discoveries of Mendel posed many problems for Darwin's theory.

Mutation is an editor, not a composer.

The probability of the production of a new gene or protein is astronomically small. With the amount of time they are giving us it's not even close to enough time to even make this a possibility. Even with billions of years if you took a single phrase and mixed up that phrase and added random letters onto it you couldn't get a complete library.

Richard Dawkins had a computer program recreate a phrase but this does not really mirror natural selection because **natural selection isn't given a phrase to look for**.

Before any beneficial protein gene folding by way of random natural selection, functional benefits would long be lost.

Chapter 11 goes over a guy who allowed an article that questioned evolution to be peer-reviewed and published in an academic journal - the guy was promptly fired.

Evolutionists make claims about genes evolving which are as unsupported as alchemists lead turning into gold.

Evolutionists make claims about gene mutation very similar to taking a book, rearranging its paragraphs randomly, rechanging the spelling of words, reordering the page number, the page arrangement etc., and expecting a more advanced book to be made from this random process.

Note - Remember: evolution is all about natural selection, which means things will naturally, left to themselves, do this stuff. Nature dissembles, it destroys. Only supernatural God creates.

Evolutionary biologists use the term de novo to refer to unexplainable sudden changes. (New terms don't solve problems.)

Evolutionists don't bring up mathematical probabilities of things they propose. Evolutionary scientists have tried to find ways around the mathematical statistical problem but are now beginning to face the facts.

You can't swap jeans around like Lego bricks.

Meyer points out various animals with specific features that could not have evolved gradually.

Evolutionists oversimplify the mathematical probability of evolution by oversimplifying organisms, oversimplifying mutations, oversimplifying how things were made, oversimplifying what a mutation can do, oversimplifying everything and ignoring the fact that many systems require multiple parts to be assembled at once.

Given the current age of Earth there's not enough time for

one single gene to evolve, much less an entire series of evolutions making animals and humans.

Evolutionists come up with wildly imaginative scenarios and on the rare occasion when they attempt to put them to the test, the tests fail.

The types of mutations that do occur are not the types of mutations required by macroevolution.

There's no sufficient variation, which means there can be no sufficient selection which means there can be no evolution of species.

Neo-Darwinism does not account for the genetic or epigenetic origins of life. Meyer goes into detail on these subjects.

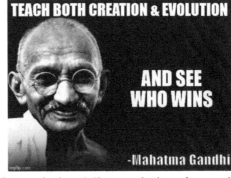
TEACH BOTH CREATION & EVOLUTION

AND SEE WHO WINS

-Mahatma Gandhi

The Cambrian explosion remains a profound problem for evolution. Microevolution observed in nature only explains survival of the fittest, not arrival of the fittest.

Neo-Darwinism depends on three claims.
1. that there are variations
2. that natural selection selects among those variations and
3. that favored variations survived to future generations.
They are variation, natural selection, and heritability. This is the triad of evolution.

Evolutionists proposed wild-eyed theories without giving any chemical or biological explanation of how those could be feasible.

Any self-organizing components in chemistry are extremely basic, nowhere near the complexity of DNA. Scientists admit that **self-organization is really more a slogan** than a theory.

Note - the Jurassic Park line "life finds a way" is just another pro-evolution slogan trying to suggest that major things can happen naturally without supernatural direction or supernatural creation.

Genes do not and cannot generate new epigenetic information.

Darwinists are in trouble when you point out that natural selection wouldn't allow for much variety, so how you going to get all the variety? Darwinists have tried to talk about various non-working gene duplication etc. theories but are stuck with this problem. It makes their time for random mutations much longer, once again excluding evolution as a possibility in the time frame we are given by modern scientists.

Scientists admit that evolution is speculative.

The whole point of natural selection theory is to explain design without designer.

Note - why do people who believe God used evolution accept evolutionary timetables? Those are timetables which would supposedly be required if no designer was involved.

It's not just that nature does not look like it evolved, nature **specifically looks like it was designed**.

Computer simulators of evolution have a target sequence, but natural evolution should not have a target sequence. Natural selection lacks foresight. Generic mutation simulators need to have a forward-looking direction, and this is precisely what nature and natural selection do not have.

Interdependent logical interactions show design (not natural selection, which is the heart of evolution theory).

See The Anarchist Manifesto.

The Cambrian explosion does not support the Darwinian idea of a bottom-up evolution.

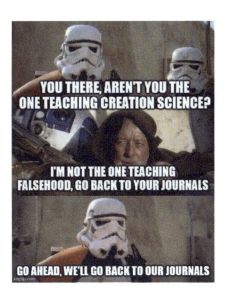

Agassi (a contemporary of Darwin) pointed out that in the fossil record, we see various prototypes which indicate intelligent design. All these years later that still appears to be the case.

The book "The invisible Man" by GK Chesterton is about how someone was murdered while four honest guards did not detect the murder. It was the mailman who clearly walked up and into the house and back out - they just didn't suspect him.

This is like how **nature clearly shows** an intelligent designer - it's just that the scientists are **unwilling to acknowledge** the designer.

The commitment to materialism in science causes them to reject intelligent design. It's not that materialism is what the evidence shows, it's **their only allowed framework**, even when the evidence points elsewhere (great full quote here if you can find it).

Scientists have **decided by fiat** to exclude anything involving intelligent design and this is greatly hindering scientific progress, **limiting the types of theories that are tested**, etc.

We shouldn't be committed to abstract criteria about whether something is scientific or not. **There are disagreements about what science is. Rather we should focus on whether something is true.**

There are unobservable things like magnetic fields etc., and gravity force, yet those are clearly science, so why is intelligent design by an unseen designer not considered scientific?

Note – and yes, we can detect the impact of God, just like we can detect the impact of gravity, magnetism, etc.

Similar logic and reasoning are used for intelligent design and Neo-Darwinism, yet they come to two different conclusions.

Experience shows us that things are made by cause-and-effect design, so why wouldn't nature be the same?

We have sufficient evidence to say causal design made nature, though we don't have all the details of how, and this is logical.

They used to think there was junk DNA, that much of the genome was not necessary because it was leftover trial and error from evolution's natural selection; now they are finding there is no junk DNA. See the Endcode Project.

Evolution's monopoly on science today stifles discussion.

Scientific materialism followed (Note- we might say 'is the fruit of') Darwinism, claiming that there is no purpose in life, no purpose for Earth, etc.

Neo-Darwinism specifically denies that natural selection is guided in any way. They say the appearance of design is an **illusion**.

You can't insist that science and religion are two separate fields and at the same time call for harmonization of science and religion.

Note: great point, Either they work together making one connective truth, or one of them is wrong.

"Why attempt to reconcile traditional Christian theology with Darwin's theory as Collins tries to do if the theory itself has begun to collapse?"

The new atheism is built on top of (note- or 'is the fruit of') Darwin's theory.

Intelligent design doesn't insist that there wasn't something before Earth and what we see was designed.

Note – these matches teachings of the restoration, that God built from existing materials, and that God isn't the first God (there is no first God).

Intelligent design shows life can have a purpose, there can be a god.

Intelligent design **detects and identifies** creation, it doesn't just say there's a designer. The ability to detect design brings science and faith into **real harmony**. This prevents feelings of anxiety and promotes feelings of wholeness and hope. We need landmarks and steady points of reference. We need a father to call out to for help when we are troubled.

Intelligent design has faith affirming implications.

By Design: Behe, Lennox, and Meyer on the Evidence for a Creator on Hoover Institution – Lecture Highlights

https://youtu.be/rXexaVsvhCM

The Cambrian explosion and other times in the geologic record show that birds appear suddenly reptiles appear suddenly fish appear suddenly there's no intermediate species.

Findings are going away from Darwin not towards him because we are finding more unique animals not animals with similar intermediate species.

In the fossil record an animal appears stays and then disappears upon extinction or survives to today.

Just opening a niche after a mass extinction does not mean new species are going to be created because there's no code for them.

Evolution does not answer the question of the original life; it claims that life has changed, but it doesn't explain how life started.

Life cannot have originated on Earth, mathematically there's not enough time even for evolution.

In Darwin's day they did not know cells were very complex, they looked like little bobs of jelly; today we know cells are run by many complex machines. In their simplistic view of nature, they thought it was reasonable for natural selection to evolve life. But it isn't reasonable. It's WAY too complex.

Judgement Day: Intelligent Design on Trial by NOVA - Highlights & Analysis

A Dover Pennsylvania school district had science teachers read a 1-minute statement saying intelligent design (ID) is an alternative to evolution. That life is too complex to evolve on its own, and that evolution's theories have lots of holes. Many science teachers and parents became angry about this and sued the school saying that the school was pushing religion. The science teachers refused to read the one-minute ID possibility statement required by the board! Court trials ensued. Currently it is considered a violation of rights to teach ID!

The evolutionists in the presentation said ID is just an attempt to push religion. They said they value their theory more than mere facts (what!?). They spoke of how evolution is much more than a theory to them, and how doubting evolution to them would be like saying the US Civil War never occurred (so much for it being a theory). They talk about the "theory of gravity" – wait, isn't it the "law" of gravity? Yep, because we have specifically demonstrated it over and over, unlike evolution of species (and no one can even define species, because they don't want to be exposed when we show that

one species can't cross into another)! The evolutionists in the presentation claim that nothing has disturbed the theory of evolution for 150 years. This is ultimate pride. How can these scientists be unaware of the scores of errors in this theory and make such a pompous statement? Ultimately the evolutionists, of course, won the case.

The ID advocates in the presentation said they wanted both evolution and ID taught to give the students fair exposure to both theories. George W Bush was in favor of intelligent design being taught at schools as another theory to be presented. (Good for Bush!) Of course, the presentation did a terrible job of presenting the ID view, not really talking about any evidence of ID, but mostly just featuring ID people talking about how upset they are. They put on quite the show demonstrating the blundering horrors of the twisted creationists (obviously threats and vandalism are uncalled for, but why focus on that?), while leaving the evolutionists enthroned, not showing flagrant deception perpetrated by their hand. This bias even in this documentary on a two-sided battle is not surprising as NOVA themselves are of course dogmatic evolutionists, as all mainstream "scientific" establishments are these days. A few cases for ID were presented by Michael Behe, author of Darwin's Black Box, such as the flagellum motor and other things which have **irreducibly complex parts**, meaning parts that if removed the whole system doesn't work, and therefore cannot form through gradual evolution. Of course, NOVA gives the evolutionists plenty of time to throw things at this, as the majority of the presentation gives time to evolution rather than ID.

Analysis:

The real issue is that we have misunderstood the separation of church and state for a long time now. It wasn't meant to mean state should be free from religion, as in only atheist. It was meant to not have the state push a certain church as the only true church. Saying that intelligent design is one of various scientific theories is in no way violating separation of church and state.

Science should be concerned with pointing out flaws in all theories. If evolution doesn't hold water, they should drop it. Unfortunately, conspiring leaders dogmatically and militantly drive evolution. Ironically, atheism has become the state religion, and no dissenting views are tolerated. It's a vertical wall in the academic journals and peer review process when you try to publish anything that isn't in line with evolution. These professional pharisees don't dare put their name on the line by getting involved.

One flaw in the theory of evolution includes the tree of life which has many gaps. The tree is shown a few times in the presentation. There is no tree! There are some similar species, but no continuous flow of one species to the next, culminating in the evolution of the human.

One flaw of the ID theory (it's more of a tenant of popular creationism in particular than intelligent design) is that limiting idea that the creation took place in 7 days, when the Bible itself says that 1000 years to man is a day to God, meaning a 7000-year creation is wholly possible within the parameters of the 7-day narrative of the Bible. The critics of ID always talk about a ridiculous 7-day creation, when ID is not even necessarily limited to that! It could be either way, but evidence I've seen points to the 7000-year creation over the 7 day version.

Intelligent Design resources mentioned in the presentation:
Textbook: Of Pandas and People: The Central Question of Biological Origins, 2nd Ed.
Darwin's Black Box by Michael Behe
Discovery Institute: a major organization in favor of intelligent design
DVD: Unlocking the Mystery of Life
Book: Darwin on Trial by Phillip E. Johnson
Movie: "Inherit the Wind" is an old movie retelling the account of a Tennessee teacher fined for teaching evolution

at school back in the day. They portray the evolutionists as sophisticated and the ID advocates as backwards hillbillies, which obviously is biased. One value of this movie might be in simply demonstrating to youth that there is debate, that it's not all one sided as modern schools portray.

Book: Traipsing into Evolution by the Discovery Institute, responding the Dover case.

EVOLUTION IS SUPPORTED BY 1000'S OF SCIENTISTS!

GEOCENTRISM WAS SUPPORTED BY 1000'S OF SCIENTISTS.

The Politically Incorrect Guide to Darwinism by Jonathan Wells PhD – Book Highlights & Commentary

My notes here only scratch the surface to many awesome concepts from this book. Be sure to learn more from this book and other volumes in the stellar "Politically Incorrect Guide" series.

Darwinism is accepted now based on popular opinion rather than evidence. It's the 'scientific consensus.'

People claim that Darwinism is Central to all the life sciences, but it's not been involved in genetics etc. Mendel did not like Darwinism. The contributions in the fields of agriculture genetics etc. have not had anything to do with Darwinism. We can have a new verb "to Darwin." When something gets stolen it's been "Darwined." Identity theft? You've been Darwined. Someone else taking credit for work you did? You've been Darwined.

Note – I remember hearing about a doctor who said you don't need to study evolution to be a good doctor, he got fired as I recall.

Darwinists shut people down who point out that Darwinism isn't a fact. One school put in a textbook that evolution is a theory not a fact and should be carefully considered before accepting. Darwinists pulled some strings and got a court to demand they remove such instructions.

Note – Darwinists love to make the word 'theory' sound like the greatest thing ever. The problem is that theories are supposed to describe how laws work, and we can't identify which laws Darwinism is trying to defend. And we all must confess that evolution is not a law. They also like to refer to evolution as an 'established' theory.

Darwin said the strongest evidence for his theory was embryos and the embryos he had drawn for his book were forgeries. Darwinists often admit that they were fudged to fit the theory but claim that they still represent truth. Academic dishonesty like this in other any other field wouldn't stand a chance. In reality, human and animal embryos in beginning stages look very different, and the beginning stages are the most important even according to Darwinists.

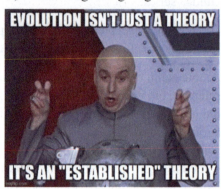

The World isn't old enough to get all the gene strands needed to make an organism by chance. If possible, it would take trillions and trillions and trillions and trillions of years.

Note - of course this is why they're always making the Earth and universe older. The more we show their theories impossible the older they make it to forestall their doom.

Michael Behe and others trying to publish intelligent design academic papers in science journals are denied. They say it's not scientific because it's not published in journals, and they won't publish it because it's not scientific (because it can't be found in academic journals). Journals also refused to publish Behe's rebuttals to those who have published attacks against him in journals. *Note – this is circular reasoning.*

Our Earth is suitable for life, and they claim our universe is just lucky enough among many universes, but there's absolutely no proof or evidence that other universes exist.

Wells gives repeated examples of how academic freedom only applies to politically correct ideas. Intelligent design advocates are not allowed to participate in various science forums, conferences etc.

The Smithsonian was going to have a show where they talked about evolution and drew a philosophical opinion from it that the cosmos might be designed for a reason. Evolutionists everywhere were outraged and got the Smithsonian to cancel the show. The Smithsonian said they decided to cancel the show because upon further analysis they concluded that such a show would not be in keeping with the mission of the Smithsonian. The Smithsonian is fine with mixing in philosophy with their science when it comes to philosophies that say there is nothing in the universe and we are all there in the cosmos, but if you ever want to promote a philosophy or even suggest the possibility of a philosophy that there might be something of design in the universe and purpose, they don't allow that. On a funny note, when the Smithsonian was considering airing this show, one evolutionist tried bribing the Smithsonian $20,000 to not play the film. A critic of evolution heard about this, called the guy, and threatened to show the film in Europe unless he paid him $20,000 also.

Microscopic living organisms have essential individual components which if removed, the whole system would fail. This is called irreducible complexity. What Darwin thought was a little black spot of an eye is extremely complex. (Michael Behe talks about this in his book "Darwin's Black Box.")

Scientists blame the religious for holding on to their religion dogmatically, but Darwinists hold on to Darwinism dogmatically. The government considers it blasphemy to question evolution.

Many have recognized that Darwinian evolution has been the **greatest contribution to atheism** the world has ever seen.

Evolution says that any gods worth having don't exist.

Intelligent design advocates don't just give rebuttals to Darwinism, they demonstrate that many things found in nature show obvious design. That many things don't work without design.

Darwinists say, 'intelligent design isn't science because it isn't testable, and besides it's been tested and found false.' (More circular reasoning.)

ONE DOES NOT SIMPLY
PUBLISH EVIDENCE AGAINST EVOLUTION IN ACADEMIC JOURNALS

Teaching students for and against creationism is not the same thing as teaching intelligent design.

Evolutionists freak out whenever someone who believes in intelligent design is hired as a science professor, even when those science professors aren't teaching intelligent design to their students, they're just pursuing and teaching that in their private life and at home.

Darwinists don't want critical analysis; they ban creationists trying to do so.

Should teachers be permitted or encouraged or required to point out problems in Darwinian evolution? Should teachers be permitted or encouraged or acquired to teach intelligent design as an alternative?

There is dispute among evolutionary biologists about all forms of life coming from a common ancestor. Nevertheless, Darwinists try to shut down intelligent design advocates from even presenting that side by saying there is 'no controversy' that 'everyone agrees' on Darwinism.

Occasionally a biology textbook will bring up intelligent design only to say that there's no evidence for it and that it's just based on the Bible. But of course, they don't let students view any of the materials defending intelligent design scientifically.

In the early 2000s Kansas took macroevolution out of their biology curriculum. Evolutionists got together and made it so those high school credits wouldn't count towards graduation.

Note – so much for localized education determined by parents. Everything is being federalized, globalized, and it's not you who gets to call the shots, it's someone smarter and more important than you. Someone who has moved beyond the primitive ways of religion and parental rights.

Kansas and Ohio in the early 2000s were debating whether to allow intelligent design to be taught as an alternative in schools. Intelligent design advocates like Stephen Meyer and the author of this book Jonathan Wells advocated allowing teachers to teach both the pros and cons of evolution theory and to not ban alternative theories.

A public high school teacher named Dehart mentioned the possibility of intelligent design in his school, and the school board approved of it. He didn't put forth his opinion, he just pointed out that there's another possibility, and the ACLU crushed him, ending his career as a public teacher.

One lady said God told her to get creation science out of the school. And nobody had a problem with that. But if she had said God told her to put creation science in the school, or that God told her to get Darwinism out of school, a lawsuit surely would have followed.

Give Darwin only praise or you face the wrath of the judiciary. Teachers must teach Darwinism, the whole Darwinism and nothing but Darwinism. What happened to the truth, the whole truth and nothing but the truth?

Darwinism has been used to justify social evils such as eugenics and racism. Darwinists put a pygmy man Ota Benga in a zoo as a display of monkeys becoming humans. He remained on display until a Baptist preacher protested at this racism and he was let free. Shortly later he killed himself.

President Bush said both sides, Darwinism and intelligent design, should be taught.

Most successful businesses rely on the Bible, not the origin of species. To be creative is to take leaps of faith. All creative thought is based on belief and is religious.

Hitler excused mass extermination based on Darwinian ideas.

Before Darwin science and religion got along well. But Darwin declared war on traditional Christianity.

A key tenant of Darwinism is that man is an accident.

Famous Darwinist Richard Dawkins said Christianity is a disease.

Several States endorse religious Darwinist views and none other.

Critical analysis of Darwin is now illegal in public schools

The Soviets persecuted scientists who taught Mendelian genetics instead of Darwinism.

Wells points out many cases of professors who dared suggest intelligent design as a possibility who got sacked.

Everyone who's been paying attention knows that there is a debate between Darwinism and intelligent design. A tactic that Darwinists are using is to claim there is no debate and that it's concluded. Anyone who knows American history knows that telling people they are not allowed to talk about something is the least likely tactic to work.

Note – we have lost much of that spirit of freedom, but I believe some of it remains with a remnant of us.

Darwinists are on the defense and their behavior shows it.

The journal Nature said that **even though all evidence points towards design, we exclude that possibility** because it is not naturalistic.

Note – this causes the modern science world to go looking for answers to questions which nature has already answered in strange places, leaving them to come up with strange scenarios to explain what should have been obvious. They become fake, looking for non-design explanations, rather than just admitting that design occurred.

Orson Scott Card *(note- a latter-day saint)* points out how Darwinist methods are unscientific and based on their supposed authority. That they resort to credentialism and expertism. But real science doesn't reject legitimate questions just because the person

the person who asked the question doesn't have certain credentials. **Resorting to credentials shows that you don't have an answer,** and you just want the questioner to go away. Expertism is to say, 'trust us you poor fools.' Darwinists tell the general public we are too dumb to understand.

Evolutionists continue to embarrass themselves by being emotional and out of control in their response to critiques and questions of intelligent design. They're not acting scientifically, they're acting dogmatically.

The arrogance being exhibited by Darwinists is the classic attitude of a loser. **The only question is whether they will go down gracefully or kicking and screaming, censoring and denouncing to the bitter end**.

Darwinism is funded with multi-billions of dollars a year by compulsory taxation. The very small intelligent design movement is funded very modestly all by donation.

Most intelligent design research must be done in secret not because it is unethical but because if Darwinists find out about it, they will shut it down. Many people involved in intelligent design research to someone secret because they would lose their job if people knew.

Intelligent design is not based in the Bible, and it is not based in America. Its popularity is growing worldwide.

Science can never be decided by judicial fiat. Darwinists may control what we are able to say, but they can't control what we think. **A major scientific revolution is at hand**, all the signs are here - forcing the opposition into silence etc.

A few more notes, these specifically from Chapter 1 on Wars and Rumors:

Darwinism claims that design is just an illusion.

Intelligent design is not a biblical theory, it is a scientific theory based on nature and logic.

Often Darwinists claim to be just peddling change over time, but they're really getting at much more.

Evolutionists claim that the attack against evolution is a war on everything, and that intelligent design would ruin everything.

Change ACROSS species (speculative)

Change WITHIN species (demonstratable)

Note – the evolutionists certainly have their tentacles in just about everything these days, but clearly this mindset is an overreaction. As evidenced by "Big History" and related projects, evolution-based thinking is a cancer that won't stop growing, infecting all of academia.

The 2005 Time Magazine had an addition on the controversy of evolution and pictured God pointing to an ape.

Change over time is simply history. It is obvious. Darwinian evolution is much different than simply change over time. Darwinism suggests change across species but what has been observed is only change within species. **Changing gene frequencies and descent modification are obvious but they don't happen across species**. Genesis said God created certain kinds.

Darwinism claims
1. all living things are descendant of a common ancestor,
2. that undirected natural selection is the principal agent causing speciation and

3. that unguided processes are sufficient to explain all living things, and whatever appears to be designed is an illusion.

Darwin said he wanted all beings as descendants of a few beings from the distant past. He said natural selection is the most important means of modification

Darwin speculated that life started in a warm little pond. Darwinism does not explain the original life. Everything before bacteria is conjecture.

Darwin said he could see no evidence of design of any kind. He saw everything as a matter of chance. Darwinists teach that man is an accident.

Evolutionists call biology the study of living things that *appear* to have been designed.

Note – maybe the recent removal of human anatomy/physiology from high school biology curriculum is due to the hand of God being so clearly evident in the human body. Russel M. Nelson, heart surgeon, said that anyone who has studied the human body has seen God moving in His majesty and power.

Intelligent design relies on evidence, so it is not religious.

Even Darwin suggested it was a possibility that God created the first or the few first living things. Today Darwinists do not allow that.

Note – when it comes to censoring God, the Devil just needed his foot in the door, and he took it from there.

It was Christian clergyman who pioneered the study of modern geology.

There has been disagreement among creationists about whether Earth is old or young, about whether God created everything at once or whether he set up programs and let them go, or how long the length of a day of creation is.

Note - my view is that each day of creation was a thousand years, and it is based on evidence and scripture. But I do see some possibility in the 24-hour creation day as well. The book of Moses also says the creation account in scripture only referring to our local area. I believe God's creations are ongoing – His works never cease. I believe His miraculous intervention in the lives of His children is a daily supernatural out-of-the-ordinary occurrence.

The new war is not about evolution and creation, it is about Darwinism and intelligent design.

Intelligent design says that some features of the natural world are best explained by an intelligent cause rather than accidental happenstance.

Design inferences are based on evidence, not just based on ignorance of how something works.

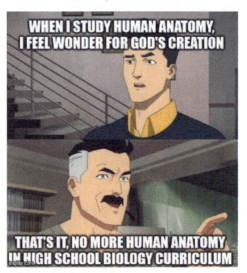

Ark in the Darkness Documentary Highlights

The ark structure is ideal, large ships today have similar structures.

Only about 7000 animals would have to be on the ark.

The flood word in Hebrew is "mabul," it appears only twice, as in the flood of Noah, and in Ps. 29:10 which says God sat as king at the flood.

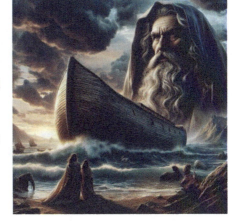

Gen. 6 has 60x repeated words like "all" and "every," showing Noah's flood was a global flood.

A local flood couldn't last that long.

If the flood was local the ark would not have been needed, all the animals would not have needed to be on it, and Noah's family could have just walked away.

Note – if it was a local flood, the covenant to never repeat such would be violated repeatedly by now.

The judgement on mankind was great "on the earth," so it wasn't a local flood. (Note – the covenant was established with Noah because he was the last man standing.)

A local judgement in the past means the future Jesus would

be local. No, both are worldwide (according to the scriptures).

You can't find Eden because it's buried under 1000s of feet of sediment. The pre-flood world was destroyed.

Mainstream scientists accept there was a global flood on now dry Mars, but they refuse it for Earth, despite Earth being already most under water. Earth is 70 percent covered in water.

Note – this is clearly out of atheistic motives.

In phase 1 of the flood the mid ocean ridge bulges up, water goes up a mile, then a tsunami from that occurs as it erupts.

If trenches weren't so deep and some mountains less high, our world would all be underwater today.

Antonio Pelegrene, a Christian, came up with continental drift decades before Wegener. Antonio cited Genesis, that at the creation there was only 1 continent.

Mid-Atlantic ridges are scars from where the great deep opened.

Each large tsunami would bring another layer of sediment. These tsunamis could cover entire continents.

Dinosaurs are found in fossil beds with thousands of animals. There aren't erosion channels (indicating rivers); a powerful flood would have killed them.

There are trees spanning several layers, which layers are supposedly millions of years apart. The Grand Canyon layers could have been deposited in a mere year.

Sea creature fossils are mixed with land creatures, they all were swept together in the flood.

Earth is mostly of water-formed sedimentary rock layers.

Bended and folded rock could only occur if the layers were soft and pliable at their formation. **Bottom layers still had to be saturated with water without time to dry out.**

Trees can't stay in contact for millions of years to be buried a little at a time, they would decompose.

Fossil trees are missing their root systems because they were transported in tsunamis and being bottom heavy, they sank bottom down and were buried thus standing.

Sedimentary layers span entire continents, showing they were formed at the same time. Sediment from the east is found in the west.

Complete rapid burial is needed for fossilization. This suggests cataclysmic events. There are trillions of fossils. Yet normally dead things decompose into dust.

Water percolated into flood sediment, bringing needed minerals for fossilization.

Note – remember we are dealing with massive amounts of sediment being shot up from the 'fountains of the deep.'

Wasp fossils are seen with open wings and legs in flight position - they were flying to escape and were trapped. We have fossils of fish-eating other fish. Fossilization was rapid and catastrophic!

All layers have saltwater creatures.

Asteroids causing dust and climate change death wouldn't bury the dinosaurs. The asteroid was invented 40 years ago when their previous theory didn't work.

Note – many scientists are beginning to admit that flooding caused extinction of the dinosaurs. Yep, it was Noah's flood!

Volcanism and water are what Genesis says happened in the flood of Noah killing all the animals. Volcanic openings from ocean floors. But secular humanists just say it was meteor impact.

Box turtles, ducks, boa constrictors, all 7 groups of animals have been found with the dinosaurs. **Museums won't show modern animals in dinosaur displays**. They want you to think these animals didn't co-exist, but that evolution occurred.

Soft tissue in dinosaur bones smelling of purification are recent discoveries that mainstream science doesn't want to get out. These dinosaur bones have elastic material and muscle tissue and red blood cells on them. These can't be old, 100,000 years tops, yet these are supposed to be tens of millions of years old. 16 types of biogenic material are found on these dinosaur bones. *(Note – it's not just bacteria that got on the bone like some scoffers are claiming.)* Collagen lasts .001% as long as evolution requires. Scientists publishing this get fired for promoting religious views, but it's just publishing scientific evidence.

*Note – evolution strikes again! If your findings contradict that narrative, they'll be **buried until we 'emerge' from the dark age of evolution**!*

Dragon legends are about the remaining dinosaurs who were hunted.

Science proves a genetic bottleneck of human population as we would see from Noah's family repopulating earth.

There are about 200 flood traditions, very similar to the Bible account. A family surviving on a boat from a flood from God. These traditions are even from places far from the ocean.

Genesis 1-11 takes place before mankind scattered, and people have legends of these shared events of creation, the flood, then the tower of Babel.

The tower of Babel was a one world government building project which God stopped by confusing the languages.

There's only one race, we are all from Adam. This inspires love for all.

Language families lead to dead ends. This contradicts the 'emerged' evolutionary language idea. Languages trace back to the time of the tower of Babel.

There were 70 Nation groups at the time of the tower of babel, and there are that many root languages.

People were surprised at the flood, and the second coming of Jesus will mirror this surprise. The flood was a judgement similar to what will come.

Public square teachings are against marriage and promote all forms of sexual deviation.

The Bible has recorded predicted events which happened exactly as it was predicted. Jesus came to earth in the only time all the prophecies about the Messiah could be fulfilled.

The sin of one man brought death to all. Sinlessness of one man brings life to all.

There was only 1 door into the ark, and there's only 1 way to salvation, which is Jesus Christ.

See Dr. John Baumgardner, Dr. Andrew Fabich, Dr. Gabriella Haynes, Dr. Mark Horstemeyer, Dr Charles

Jackson, Dr. Terry Mortenson, Dr. Randall price, the Logos research Association, Dr. Andrew Selling, Dr. Carl Werner.

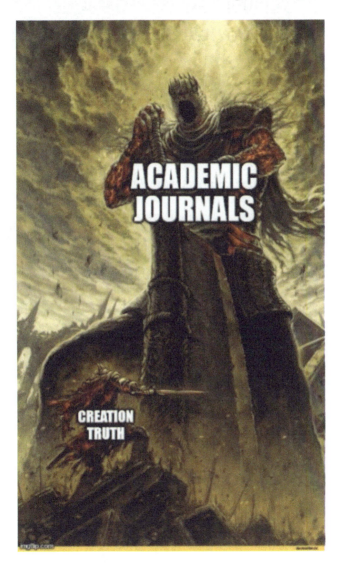

Dragons or Dinosaurs? Creation or Evolution? By Darek Isaacs – Documentary Highlights & Commentary

Produced by Cloud Ten Pictures

These notes are in my own words and do not represent all the ideas in the presentation.

See
https://www.youtube.com/watch?v=zgLDE_6TepM

The word dinosaur was invented after the Bible was published. They use jackal now instead of dragon because of fear of evolutionists, but the word should be translated as dinosaur based on the descriptions of historians.

There is much lore of dragons across cultures.

One Indian legend said a giant bird would bring thunder when it visited them. The bird lived in the mountaintops. We see for a bird to live in the mountain tops it would need the updraft from a thunderstorm to get there, hence the Indians said it was a bird which brought lightning.

Many things that were around in the supposed age of dinosaurs are still here today like Oak and other trees.

Water deposited sediment is where we find most fossils. Such is like Noah's flood time, when sudden massive amounts of water come. Most bones are very scattered since when they fall to the floor of the ocean they are devoured. Also, calcium carbonate is soluble in sea water. Hence, forming fossils is a rare thing to happen.

Note: But the near complete skeletons, and many in an area, indicate rapid burial.

Mt. Saint Hellens made many layers of sediment not taking 100's of years to form, but one day. This surprised geologists.

Measure current lava flow from Hawaii and you won't get 0 years old, but ancient.

Radioactive decay rates have been at increased rates in certain periods of history as one study called RATE shows.

The presentation goes over evidence for the earth being about 6000 years old. (about 50min in).

Note – Earth could be 13k with a 7k creation, applying the 1:1000 ratio that appears several times in scripture. Either way, it's a finite short amount of time, not the fantastical millions of years dreamed up by evolutionists to attempt to justify, or rather mask, their godless claims.

Lava flow in a canyon (that is younger than the canyon) is measured as older than the canyon. More C14 discussion is presented.

The presentation goes over dinosaur bones found with blood cells in it; this is fresh marrow with soft blood vessels. This could not be if that animal died many years ago!

Charles Lyell said, "I am sure you may get into Q.R. what will **free the science from Moses**, for if treated seriously, the party are quite prepared for it." (June 14 letter to George

Poulett Scrope)

These teachings brought on statements such as, "Lyell saw himself as **"the spiritual saviour of geology**, freeing the science from the **old dispensation of Moses**." (Porter, Roy S. (July 1976). "Charles Lyell and the Principles of the History of Geology". *The British Journal for the History of Science*. **32** (2): 91–103.)

Were life to go from microbes to man, it would take more like googol years than billions of years; evolutionists saying billions of years is a way of saying an impossible thing can happen.

They say over billions of years anything is possible, but would you claim a person could win the lottery daily for 100 years? This is the type of claim evolutionists make.

Evolutionists say the simplest life was long ago, like a jellyfish, but they actually have about as much DNA as we do. (Not so simple, are they.)

If you want to say things are by chance in being formed, what is the difference between billions of years vs. thousands of years?

There should be millions of species between others in evolution, but there is not. Darwin's stages of animals etc. are no longer what we use.

Newton, Boyle, Maxwell, Faraday, Carver, Pasteur, all these were Christian Bible believing people. They have helped open us to more science than most.

Job 40 says, "I made (this beast of beasts) **along with you**." Some Hebrew experts say it was the largest land animal God made. It was said to have a tail like a Cedar tree. Consider the Cedars of Lebanon, they are huge. Another place says arms like great bars of iron.

Job 41 Leviathan is described as leaving a trail in the mud that shatters pots, etc. God describes that it has layers of shields with no gaps between them, and that it breaths fire. There is a beetle that shoots hot liquid at things, the electric eel that electrocutes, the cobra that shoots poison into the eye. There is a hollow part in the dinosaurs with an unknown function, it could be for mixing chemicals to make fire.

Were dinosaurs on the ark of Noah? The average size of dinosaur is that of a goat. Animals were on the boat so they could reproduce. Science today teaches they could reproduce at age 8 to 10, so young dinosaurs would be brought. Many of them would have been wiped out by the flood.

There are legends of hunting dragons; that is one way there are fewer of them.

The ice age after the flood of Noah could have killed many dinosaurs also.

Note – there's lots of ice age theories, ranging from many to none.

Many think of how we come into existence randomly without a creator so they don't have to be accountable to a creator. When Christ comes evolutionary theory will utterly go away.

Evolutionary theory is driven by paradigms, not by evidence.

The Appellation and Himalayan mountains were made from the flood. There are fossils in it because animals were crushed in that in the flood.

Note – another theory is that the waters went high above these mountains.

Today one of the biggest reasons they can't believe in Jesus is because of what they teach in science class in school; **based on what they teach in school, the Bible does not make sense**!

Today's science is proving that processes that were thought to take millions of years can be done in very short periods of time. (Note – this is true from fossilization to coal formation to layer deposition to canyon formation etc.)

Man's views and opinions are always changing; rest your hopes and views on God's wisdom, not man's.

Forensic scientists don't see crimes, they make conclusions and suggestions on what could have happened. The judge and jury will determine the case by the eyewitness of who fired the gun from where. This is what the Bible does for us.

Is Genesis History? Documentary Highlights

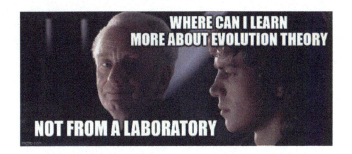

These are my notes on the presentation, and do not exactly capture the ideas presented. As they are extensive, permission has been obtained to share them from the author. As is typical, I don't agree with all the ideas put forth in this documentary but share many fascinating elements of it.

First, they cover geology, then biology, then astronomy, then history.

Genesis History: Geology

Mt. Saint Helens made geological structures which we usually attribute to being extremely old. Deep bedrock can be cut in just a few days with powerful mudslides. Catastrophic processes can make big things happen fast.

Note - see also Universal Model theory of the Grand Canyon as being formed by flood deposits followed by a major earthquake.

See Steve Austin PhD Geologist

Genesis speaks of fountains of water coming up at time of Noah's flood.

Note – evolutionists bash on creationism saying there's not enough water in the atmosphere for a worldwide flood, but we never said there was!

Mountains have risen since the flood, so we can't look at them to determine how deep the flood was.

Note – There's compelling evidence for the flood to have been around 5 miles deep, which would cover the tallest known mountains. There are other theories as well.

Note - Latter-day Saints know that the earth was baptized by immersion, completely, by the flood. Great evidence exists for this fact in science and doctrine.

The standard idea is that the Colorado river wore the Grand Canyon down over tens of thousands of years, but erosion would have collapsed it over that time. The Grand Canyon could have been eroded in just a few weeks. The Grand Canyon would have been from a large powerful flood, not just a local flood. The Grand Canyon more logically would have been made with a lot of water in a little time rather than a little water over a long time.

Science isn't just about evidence, it's about paradigms, how you interpret the evidence.

Note – Good point. Stephen Meyer in "Darwin's Doubt" points out how modern science has arbitrarily decided to refuse to consider any evidence pointing to intelligent design.

Steven Boyd PhD. Hebraist says the world's greatest Hebraists agree that Genesis is narrative, not poetic. This means that the text should be understood as it is written. The biblical text does not conform with the contemporary narrative. God creates mankind. Marriage was invented *(by God)* in the beginning of mankind. A global flood occurs. The tower of Babel text shows how different languages evolved.

Jesus descended from Adam as the Bible text genealogy shows. Mankind was created on the 6th day of creation. This shows that the days of creation could not have been extremely long ago.

Mt. St. Helens was small compared to other historic volcanic eruptions. We can't use present day rates of processes to determine how long the geological record accumulated (because there are catastrophes which aren't constantly occurring).

The millions of years of decay rate of atoms at present day doesn't mean the rate was consistent in the past. Universities ignore evidence of historic rates being different because they are set in their millions of years geological evolution idea. They insist that we have rocks millions of years old to support this narrative.

Samples from the same rock can test to be vastly different ages.

Where there are no evidence of erosion between layers, those layers were quickly laid down upon each other; this is seen in areas of the Grand Canyon.

The Grand Canyon was underwater deposition (see presentation for details).

Note – I've heard a few different ideas on this, all of which were superior to the idea of underground layer building from subduction based on slow plate movement which then slowly emerged, as mainstream science claims.

See Kurt Wise Paleontologist

The book of Peter prophecies people in the last days will say that the Lord isn't going to come because things are always going to be as they always have been. They deny the idea that the past was any different than the present.

Note – James Hutton's "Uniformitarian" theory, central to the old Earth claims, is a huge fulfillment of this scripture concerning false doctrines to be taught in the last days. Evolution is only 200 years old; it is an apocalyptic theory of doom.

The Bible describes different epochs of time where very different things happen; God starts and ends certain projects. At the time of Adam and Eve it says they would have lived forever if they had not sinned, there were different conditions. Now the sun won't burn forever, etc.

In the ante-diluvian (pre-flood) epoch, there were very different animals and plants on earth. In Peter it says that world was destroyed. (The scriptures speak of new heaven and new earth several times.)

The earth is still recovering from the flood; this can describe glacial history, etc.

The modern epoch of time based on our current observations can only describe the earth back to a few hundred years after the flood of Noah.

The Bible records historical events but it (*usually) doesn't tell how they happened; we can study nature to find out how these events happened.

Note – good point; the Bible *is true, so we clearly can find natural evidence of it, and clearly this will build faith in God. This is one of the big reasons he gave us the* Bible*!*

A great flood could have taken ocean animals and thrown them onto land continents. The Cambrian explosion (an appearance of lots of marine animals which shows up almost out of nowhere) makes sense as the flood was about destroying ecosystems; we see a complex whole explosion of life (in the fossil record, indicating mass death); whenever you move up in the geological record, you see different ecosystems. The flood waters got higher and higher and destroyed more and more, until it got to the top. In other words, all that life was already there, we are just looking at the graveyard of all that life.

Placement of the next layer on the fossil record must have been quick; entire ecosystems and species getting wiped out at the event of the worldwide flood.

At the time of the flood the earth was filled with violence; it was not so at the time of creation. When we go to natural history museums, we see the animals of the time of violence on earth. (In the beginning there weren't carnivores.)

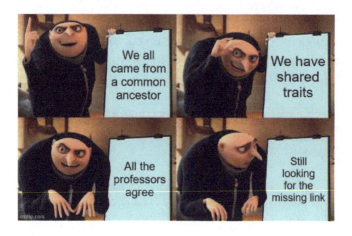

*Note – right, and the Book of Mormon reinforces this in 2 Nephi 2:22 which says there was no death before the fall of Adam, and it applies that to ALL things (not just in Eden). Then we have a millennium where things will go back to paradise, when there will **again** be no more death. (We look forward to a restoration of peace, not the first peace Earth has ever known.)*

Fossilization requires very special circumstances; if a coyote dies in the desert today, its body soon disappears. Fossilization is rare, yet we find dinosaur fossils all over the Earth.

Note - Rapid fossilization has been observed, and occurs easily when conditions are met, including high pressure etc.

The rule is that there are no transitional forms, those forms remain the same in the next stages of the fossil record; when there are transitional forms, that's the exception rather than the rule.

Genesis History: Biology

Devin Anderson PhD microbiologist speaks of what's inside dinosaur bones. There have been tissue with cells found in dinosaur fossils which are supposedly 80 millions of years old, but those should have broken down faster. Such tissue has been found in a triceratops, etc.

Note – Learn more about Mary Schweitzer's findings on dinosaur tissue at https://www.youtube.com/watch?v=0-K7_H27Wq4

See the Creation Research Society

Soak a fossil in EDTA, the tissue remains; stretchable, pliable tissue. An even closer electron scanner shows extreme details of the cells. You would not expect such elaborate detail still intact if the sample was as old as many claim. The scientific community responded to this saying it was just bacteria or other things it could be, so those who originally published this tissue finding did more research and even found proteins. The controversy has been how to explain such. Some claim it means nothing because our other methods of dating say it's older. But this tissue is a method of dating. This challenges the entire dating process.

Time is the critical component for evolution; they claim to account for massive change of organisms with *time*.

Darwin first read about a millions of years-old earth, and made his theory to fit that paradigm; he didn't come up with the millions idea.

Note – similarly, people first hear about evolution theory, then go around looking for the missing links. They didn't find evidence then make the theory, it was backwards.

Evolution is a belief that enough change over time and enough time can account for every species coming from one thing; but there are major missing links in every species. A shark is a shark, and there are variations of a shark, but even back in the fossil record you have sharks.

No one would agree that random mutations would result in a higher lifeform. The number of changes required to move from one species to another requires many changes at once.

Things do change over time, but they don't jump to different species. Several animals can be very similar within their group. Animals can have similar sets of genes, but the genes controlling the development of the embryo are very different in different species.

Look at computer programs; everything doesn't just come from a single symbol.

The 4th dimension is time; the genome changes shape over time; all 3 dimensions change in the 4th dimension. You can't build something like that one step at a time; there must be foresight, it can't be one letter at a time with natural selection. Animals were **created with the ability to change** and adapt to their environments, and we have mistaken that as evolution.

An ecosystem comes crashing down without all factors being present; remove just a few factors, and it collapses. If you have 'missing links,' you can't have a complete genome.

Each kind of animal descended from a master form which was on the ark of Noah. God didn't just build a cat; he built an animal from which a variety of cats could come. Diversity of today is built into the kind. (But not every kind came from a single common ancestor.)

Natural selection can't generate all diversity we see; natural selection does fine tuning, but it doesn't account for all the variety. Selection takes a variation and turns it into a local adaptation. An exquisite design in the beginning built into the system of an animal the ability to adapt to different climates to an extent. Each kind has its

own tree of variation. Therefore, the Genesis paradigm embraces both similarity and difference.

Note - Natural selection evolution is inherently atheistic by definition. It's natural, not supernatural. The whole point is an attempt to do away with God and purpose. What we are learning in cutting edge science is that it simply can't be done without supernatural means. Design is inherent and plainly evident.

There are discontinuities between humans and non-humans. Neanderthals are a variety of human. There are a large variety of humans like how there are a large variety of dogs. But there are discontinuities between humans and non-humans. Apes for example are very different from humans, there are large discontinuities.

70

Genesis History: Astronomy

See Danny Faulkner PhD astronomer.

Eclipses are spectacular and rare; these are part of a design for signs as the scriptures say.

Scripture said let the earth bring forth plants; it could have been rapid creation, the "bring forth" suggests that. It may have appeared like a time lapse taking place in regular time. This could be why we see light from distant galaxies. (The ideas on light having traveled billions of light-years from distant galaxies to reach us is a fabrication to hold up their theory of deep time.)

If spiral galaxies were so old, why would they still appear spiraled? They would have come together.

The Big Bang Theory is far from being universally accepted by scientists. Some claim Big Bang can be compatible with the Bible, but those are people who attempt to wed Genesis with our current paradigm. We should interpret the world in terms of Genesis, not the other way around.

Note - At BYU the evolutionary biologists terrifyingly claim that they seek to reconcile religious FAITH with scientific FACT! This of course is typical of all Christian evolutionists and thinking in general these days. Religion gets the back seat on the bus.

Genesis History: History

Douglas Petrovich PhD archeologist shows biblical events unfolding in the East at Mesopotamia. He speaks of language popping up out of nowhere, and great diversity in grammar forms of language to language even in ancient languages. (I recall in my Egyptology class we spoke of the oldest language records going back only to about 4000 BC).

Our bodies are set up for the timing of a day as evident by our sleep cycles, our work cycles, etc. The timing of the day was set up in Genesis.

If you remove a literal Adam and Eve, you greatly alter human history and it becomes open to lots of interpretation about relationships, the character of gender, sexuality, marriage, etc.

We understand the life of Christ as recorded in the Bible being historical events; why do we think that the Old Testament would not be historical events? We are constantly bombarded with the message that we must adjust our views. The entire Bible refers to all the characters of Genesis. The entire Bible is refuted if you throw out the original characters and major events of Genesis. Throw out the first few chapters of the Bible, and you must throw out the whole thing. **History anchors all the other disciplines. It tells us what happened, then science attempts to answer how those events of history happened**, the mechanics of those events. If you reverse that and have science say what happened, you get a constantly **shifting world view, and moral relativism** is the necessary outcome. God has given us the bedrock to build on by giving us the Bible. Nothing in the world makes sense except in the light of Genesis!

Scientific Creationism by Henry Morris – Book Highlights & Commentary

This is a flagship creation science volume, and my notes here only scratch the surface on a few principles from the text. I don't agree with all his claims but will point out here many fascinating findings.

Introductory Chapters (1-3)

Modern science asks the wrong questions.

The fact that we have energy from the Sun is one thing but they can't answer how that energy would have made evolution happen.

Recombination does not result in new, it's only changing around what's already there.

If someone did develop a wing or an eye it wouldn't be helpful, it would even be dangerous, and natural selection would not favor its continuance.

Darwin said the thought of how natural selection could make the eye made him ill as in he didn't think it was possible.
But he needed it to be.

There are many predictions which creation model makes which actually work, and many times things in evolution model cannot be predicted.

Mutations are rare, not common. And good mutations are extremely rare. Accidental occurrences are expected to be harmful.

Today's species are dying out not being created, so if the present is the key to the past, how do you have evolution?

Ch. 4 Accident or Plan?

A simple probability study shows the absolute impossibility of Earth and life being formed by chance.

Natural selection supposedly turns impossibilities into possibilities.

The creation model predicts that different species would be designed with similar features for similar functions, and different features for different functions. But the evolution model has a problem, namely why are cats and dogs so different if they both evolve from the same thing? If evolution were true, there would be many different kinds of part cat part dog creatures and you wouldn't be able to tell where the cat ended and where the dog began with all these species.

Seemingly similar structures in different kinds of animals and humans which are used as supposed evidence for evolution are actually better evidence for creation. For starters, the distinctions between these bone groups are arbitrarily made by us.

Morphology, similar hand structures etc., this only shows our ability to classify. It favors the creation model because not only are there similarities but there are gaps and distinct differences between species. In the evolution model you would have extremely similar species, you wouldn't be able to tell where the one started and the other ended.

Embryology proves common design. It's normal that features look similar in the beginning as various life forms have similar features like heads and limbs, and they're in a similar environment. But then they specialize into their distinct species. The differences show up fairly early and these differences attest to creation, not evolution.

There are some similarities in DNA between different living things, but the important thing is that they are different.

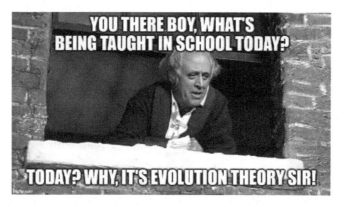

DNA is a plain witness to creation because DNA only allows for one thing to turn into that specific thing. DNA puts definite limits on how much a species can adapt.

There are similar behaviors in some living things, but the important point is that there are significant differences in behaviors.

Some animals greatly confuse evolutionists because they look like two very different kinds of animals like the whale being a mammal shaped like a fish and the independent development of wings for bats, wings for birds, wings for insects, that all of these came from a common ancestor and independently developed wings is bizarre.

Supposedly vestigial organs which we thought had no use for which evolutionists said were from evolving away from needing are now being found to have uses. The appendix etc. all these that used to be thought of as being useless they are finding the uses for. Just because the scientists weren't aware of their function doesn't mean they had none.

Human embryos never at any time develop skills or gill slits. It also has no tail or fins and never is a fish. It does develop pouches which become various glands; the pouches are guides for developing blood vessels and are not useless. The recapitulation theory that humans are first fishes in embryo then turn into humans used to be popular and evolutionists now are having to admit that it doesn't work.

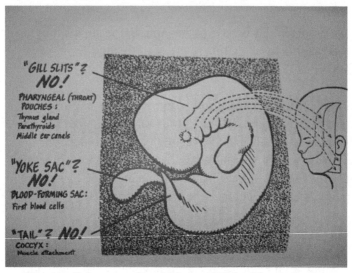

(Image: Science vs Evolution p.698 by Vance Ferrel,
EvolutionFacts.com)

The same kind of gaps exist in the fossil record as they do for present-day plants and animals. The fossil record shows clear-cut categories, not a horizontal continuum of transitional species.

The "species" level of classification is all that we can genuinely differentiate; there are clear and obvious gaps between species. Higher levels of supposed organization like "family," "class" etc. are arbitrary as you can't prove them. We don't find transitional fossils that would fit into the "class" or "order" category. The gaps between species are permanent, you're never going to find them.

There's no transitional fossil between a vertebrate and its supposed invertebrate ancestor. These two types of animals were created separately.

He speaks of a fish they thought was extinct but they found it in the Caribbean, it was embarrassing, it was a fish that supposedly had some amphibian features but here it is today and it has not become an amphibian, it's still a fish and it hasn't changed over the supposedly 100 million years from the fossil of it.

The catfish the lungfish and the walking fish were all thought to possibly be transitional, but even the evolutionists now agree that they do not qualify as transitional for various reasons.

The fact that a fossil may be hard to tell whether it was a reptile or a mammal is not evidence of it being a transitional fossil, these animals merely have similar features on the bone level.

He quotes a scientist who says there is a universal absence of transitional fossils.

Archeopteryx is not part reptile at all, it is 100% bird. It is a feathered warm-blooded animal. Whether it's birds mammals fishes or reptiles, some have teeth and some don't. The fact that archeopteryx has teeth does not indicate that it is part reptile part mammal.

Ancient fossils are often a bigger version but the same structure as the modern animal.

There are no transitional fossils for birds, no transitional fossils for insects, the list goes on and on for every type of animal.

There is no evidence for punctuated equilibrium (the idea that sudden changes occurred followed by long periods of no changing).

Ch. 5 Uniformism or Catastrophism?

He covers many rock formations continent wide which aren't forming today, and must have been from catastrophic volcanism and continent wide flooding to spread the material.

If the present is key to the past it should be obvious that all of the fossil life lived at the same time; today we have birds mammals reptiles humans single-celled organisms, all of us at the same time, and so it was for the past animals.

There is no worldwide unconformity, you can't determine where one age begins and the other ends; they use "para-conformities" which means no visible difference in the geologic layers but only a difference in fossils; but further analysis has shown that there is no way to tell by fossils of one age beginning and another ending. The record is continuous!

Invertebrates are at the bottom of the fossil layers because that's where they live, at the lower altitudes.

Humans have always lived separate from starfish and other types of animals, that's why their fossils aren't found together.

More spherical animals would settle lower because they have less drag in the flood water.

They tried to explain away dinosaur fossil prints next to human fossil prints by saying there was some kind of dinosaur with human shaped feet, which there is of course no evidence for.

Geologists are beginning to admit that geologic formations can best be explained by sudden catastrophic events, and they say there are long amounts of time between these events (punctuated equilibrium), but the only reason for claiming the long amounts of time between events is evolution theory!

Ch. 6 Old or Young: How to Date a Rock

The geologic time scale was made before radiometric dating and radiometric dating is so unreliable that it gives dramatically different dates; they throw out dates which don't match the pre-determined ages.

*Note - One professor admitted the selective use of favored radiometric dates in the scientific community when he said, "If a C-14 date supports our theories, we put it in the main text. If it does not entirely contradict them, we put it in a footnote. And if it is completely 'out-of-date,' we just drop it." (*T. Save-Soderbergh and *Ingrid U. Olsson, "C-14 Dating and Egyptian Chronology," Radiocarbon Variations and Absolute Chronology, ed. *Ingrid U. Olsson (1970), p. 35 [also in *Pensee, 3(1): 44].)*

Note - Another researcher admitted just how many unapproved radiometric dates they throw out when he said, "It may come as a shock to some, but fewer than 50 percent of the radiocarbon dates from geological and archaeological samples in northeastern North

*America have been adopted as 'acceptable' by investigators." (*J. Ogden III, "The Use and Abuse of Radiocarbon," in Annals of the New York Academy of Science, Vol. 288, 1977, pp.167-173.)*

God's chief purpose is to create and help man, so God wouldn't waste untold eons of time caring for evolutionary developments without man.

*Note- of course evolution suggests that God wasn't
involved at all. One wonders what God was doing.*

You can't know the components in a system in ancient
times. No system is closed. A closed system is just a
theoretical idea to simplify things. Since real nature is not a
closed system it can be influenced by external variables
fluctuating.

You cannot ascertain that the decay rate was constant.

All these flawed assumptions in today's dating methods
prove them unreliable. Furthermore, they only accept
dating methods which yield long eons of time, and actively
reject other methods.

Some of the daughter component may have been initially
created at the same time as the parent component.
There are many ways daughter products could be
incorporated into the systems when first formed.

No process rate is unchangeable in nature. Many factors
influence process rates, and these factors can change. Rates
are at best only statistical averages, not deterministic
absolutes.

He discusses the unreliability of uranium potassium etc. in
dating. Lead vaporization and free neutrons etc. indicate
that the lead ages, which are typically the oldest ages, could
indicate nothing whatsoever about age.

Modern formations of lava rocks are dated to be millions of

years old. When Rock melts it's supposed to reset the clock. Uranium aging on rocks of known ages is incorrect, so why should we trust uranium aging of rocks of unknown ages?

We accept the potassium dates which most closely resemble the uranium dates, but the uranium dates themselves are unreliable.

The change in argon is from the environment, not the decaying process. Environmental fluid and gaseous argon at the time of lava flow being incorporated into the igneous rock can account for the argon levels rather than supposed to decay rates.

Continental drift rates are also based on potassium argon dating of rocks on the seafloor, and are therefore flawed.

Rubidium strontium dating is also measured by uranium dating, so bad uranium methods make these unreliable too.

Rubidium strontium can easily be leached out and there are other obvious flaws.

Oldest writings are only 4,000 to 6,000 years old.

Note- my BYU Egyptologist professor John Gee told us that the oldest written records in existence only go back to around 4,000 BC! This of course fits the Bible's timeframe perfectly.

There is no substantial evidence that helium-4 can or does escape through the atmosphere in substantial amounts, therefore we are left with the current amount by which we can determine that the Earth is quite young.

Helium-4 is probably entering our atmosphere from the sun's Corona. This maximizes the age of our atmosphere at 1.75×10^5 years given a starting of zero helium in the atmosphere.

He discusses the amount of nickel on Earth limiting the Earth's age to a few thousand years, like 9,000.

Small amounts of ocean metal precipitation limit the Earth's age to several thousand years.

Dating based on the magnetic sphere limits Earth's age to around 6,000-10,000 years.

The processes most likely to be uniform would have occurred over a short amount of time and on a worldwide level; this makes something like dating via the magnetic sphere much more reliable than argon potassium.

Processes at a constant uniformitarian rate date the Earth as very young, and you can only get rid of those if you get rid of the other uniformitarian processes they use to claim Earth is old.

There are many more processes that give young ages for

Earth than processes which give old ages, and the processes that give old ages can even better be interpreted by young ages.

Living mollusks have a carbon date of 23,000 years old which indicates that there's some kind of carbon exchange taking place before death, and this goes directly against carbon dating assumptions. This makes the radiocarbon date much too big.

It has been demonstrated that carbon-14 decay rates could have varied in the past.

The amount of natural carbon could have been different in the past, which would have altered the decay ratio. If there was a significant **difference in the amount of**

Radiocarbon Dated Living Rats: -260 to 2,139 Years Old

vegetation and or the amount of volcanic carbon emissions in the past it would dramatically change the carbon dates. Vast coal deposits around the world attest to the point that they're used to be much more vegetation.

Population statistics support that humans have been on Earth for only a few thousand years, not upwards of a million as Evolution says. Even allowing for wars etc. the number of people that would likely be on earth if people had been here for upwards of a million years is absurdly high. To make Evolution work you must make major modifications to basic population statistics, but the creation model fits the data correctly without such major modifications. If so, many people had lived on the earth for so long there would be much more of a fossil record of it also.

Gravitational energy from the sun's inward collapsing process could be much more likely the cause of solar energy. In 1979 it was confirmed that the sun is shrinking and calculated that the sun must be quite young. What we know about the sun size and change of shape indicates that it would have been twice in size not long ago, which would have annihilated Earth.

Polonium halos in rocks indicate their near instant creation!

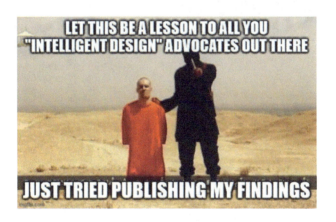

Ch. 7 Apes or Man

When they find skeletons of slightly different sized skulls

or teeth, they are quick to claim it as a hominid. Different teeth just mean different diet or habitat. Further, rickets arthritis poor diet and other medical conditions can make skeletons look different. There is significant variation in people and in monkeys; some are big, some small, etc., and this in no way is evidence of intermediate species between animals and humans.

They're finding full human skeletons in locations dated before the supposed hominids.

If all people came from a common ancestor they would have had the same language, so why would they split up so much as to cause different races? The language barrier is the main thing that keeps different races from intermarrying.

Language is an unbridgeable gulf between man and animals, our ability to communicate abstract thought. The oldest language we know is already modern sophisticated and complete.

Some animals have instinctive language but it's not language which involves learning new things and passing it on to the next generation. When animals learn how to do new things it is not transmitted to their progeny, only man has this ability, as growing civilizations attest.

Yes there are people who have lived in caves and yes, they have used stone tools, but this is not a sign of evolutionary development. There are still people doing that today, there always have been.

When the oldest cultures of an area seem to be the stone age type, this is because when people first migrated there, they were using the tools they already had, and it wasn't until they found ore bodies that they could begin mining, smelting, and resuming all their industry. Particularly after the flood you have people migrating to new areas.

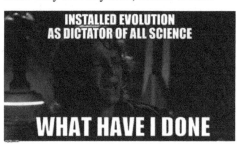

INSTALLED EVOLUTION
AS DICTATOR OF ALL SCIENCE

WHAT HAVE I DONE

He goes over many predictions of the creation model which are supported by archeology geology biology etc. but that are not supported by evolution.

The expected dates of the earliest civilization should be around 4000 BC, the only claim for older civilizations are based on radiocarbon dates.

Dendrochronology (tree ring dating) is unreliable because frequently two or more growth periods occur in the same year.

Note – but even the oldest trees aren't very old, around 10,000 years, which particularly works with the 1000-year day model as several scriptures indicate, though that model is not popular among most creationists.

Recently a human skull bone was found in Africa in a soil layer that was supposed to be over 2 billion years old.

It is an objective fact that humans are moral religious beings and animals are not.

Evolution has its own system of ethics values and ultimate meanings which makes it a religion, which makes teaching of it in public schools indoctrination. The American Humanist Association officially recognizes Evolution as a religion.

Note – if religions are going to be taught in schools, and they could be, they should be recognized, not hidden.

All of the supposed evidence for human evolution can fit

inside a single coffin. He goes over the various hominid claims which were proven false.

Note – since the time of his book they've come up with more claims, but they're just claims. They'll always come up with something or other to uphold their theory, which is another indication we aren't dealing with objective observation when it comes to evolutionary theory.

Ch. 8 Creation According to Scripture

It is now known that early man was a highly specialized technologist in many fields. There's no reason why not to believe that man could read and write from the beginning of his creation. People used to argue against the Bible claiming that people couldn't read and write back

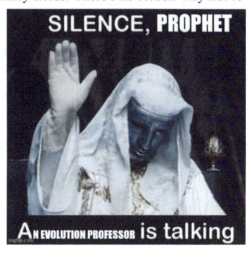

then, but now we know that's clearly false.

Jesus accepted the historicity and accuracy of Genesis. To

reject Genesis is to reject Christ.

It is probable concerning the first five books attributed to Moses that the Book of Genesis was edited by Moses and that the other four were directly written by him. The Book of Genesis is never accredited to Moses in scripture, it is likely that the Book of Genesis was written by the patriarchs of that time such as Adam Noah etc. The creation account would have either been directly written by God as were the ten commandments, or a direct Revelation from God. Either way, creation accounts in scripture give us information we could have had no other way since no mortal was there to witness it.

Note - he claims God created things from nothing, but the Latter-day Saints view creation as taking existing materials and organizing them by supernatural means.

WHO WOULD WIN?

HEALS PEOPLE INSTANTLY	WARM LITTLE POND
CREATED EARTH IN 7 DAYS	NATURAL SELECTION
SELF-EXISTENT	SURVIVAL OF THE FITTEST
OMNIPOTENT	MAYBE HOMINIDS
TELLS A STORM TO STOP	TAX FUNDING
ALLOWS AGENCY	CRUSHES OPPOSITION
RAISES THE DEAD	NO PURPOSE
OMNIPRESENT	GOD USED EVOLUTION
OMNISCIENT	NO OFFICIAL POSITION
SACRIFICES FOR ALL	ISN'T IT WONDERFUL?
FORESEES FUTURE	BILLIONS OF YEARS
SENDS PROPHETS	IMPOSSIBLY SMALL ODDS
	ON YOUR OWN

Genesis 1:7 shows that the primordial world had waters

above the firmament. The firmament overhead could have blocked radiation, allowing longer life.

Note – the firmament also could have modified the atmosphere giving a more favorable amount of oxygen, etc.

Note – evolutionists have no answer for why Adam and other ancients had significantly longer lifespans than we do today.

There would not have been fossils in the creation, that's a sign of death, which is a sign of evil. Death came into the world only with sin. God isn't responsible for death and suffering.

Note – great point. No death until the fall, so no fossils before the fall. I've also seen convincing evidence that most fossils were made in the catastrophic event of Noah's flood.

God's love is voluntary, and so must ours be. Involuntary love is a contradiction of terms.

Why energy is conserved, why entropy increases, these are explained in scripture. See his references on these.

All we see in this fallen world should remind us of our separation from God.

"After his kind" occurs 10 times in Genesis.

Scripture says, "All flesh is not the same flesh."

Claiming you can have biblical evolution is like claiming

you can have Christian atheism.

God has all power; he can create without eons.

God's goal is man, why wait so long to create him?

Note - especially when we know he can procreate as much as anyone else. To say He can't is like saying the axe hefted itself, boasting that it didn't need the man (see Isaiah). Surely the creation doesn't have more power and ability than the Creator.

The Hebrew "Yom" usually means day, not time. "Olam" is the Hebrew word to indicate a long period of time. Evening and morning also are always used to mean a literal day.

Note – this is right, and limits us to our 24-hour days, or the 1000-year days God experiences, as indicated in multiple scriptures. Time is based on which planet you're on. Either model would be an excellent explanation for how this Earth was made.

Plants are made before the sun in the creation account of Genesis. For plant life to live without the sun is easy with days of creation just normal day lengths.

*Note - but another light source should work too. Either
way, evolutionists are wrong in claiming that the sun HAD
to be first.*

The 6-day work week for us is identical to the work week
of God. We are told to rest 1 in 7 as He does.

Morris goes over the many opposites of evolution and the
Bible.

They say evolution must be true, so the earth must be old.
They use this circular reasoning to reject ages which don't
match the theory.

In Exodus 20 it says God created in 6 days and rested the
7th, he wouldn't need to rest if he merely said a few
sentences. There's more to it than that.

Establishing flood geology is where creationists are
attacked most, and if we establish this, evolution falls apart.
(Note – many books have done a great job at this.)

The flood couldn't be local, to cover mt Ararat you'd need
an egg-shaped dome of water there if it were only local.

Note – some claim there were no mountains before the flood, but some creation accounts do refer to mountains being formed in the beginning. It is true however that we don't know the size of these mountains, and mountain height could have dramatically changed during the flood. I believe there were tall mountains before the flood, and that flood waters were five miles high. This was a monumental event beyond our comprehension. Several experiments have been conducted to demonstrate this fact, establishing that in these conditions of pressure bones would be easily turned virtually instantly into rock. See Universal Model 2 for details on those experiments.

Scripture says there was no rain before flood.

God's promise to never again send a flood would be broken repeatedly if it was only a local flood.

If the Bible is true at all, you must reject the geological ages.

Note – the geological ages were made in a direct attempt to overthrow the Bible. *When we understand this, it becomes increasingly silly to try and mesh the two narratives.*

God created darkness, that's how it starts.

Writing off Genesis 1-11 as not history and not scientific destroys the whole Bible.

Darwin's Black Box by Biochemist Michael Behe – Book Highlights & Commentary

Introductory Note: This was an excellent book demonstrating the complexity of biological systems, and how absurd it would be to believe that they evolved by chance natural selection. Biological organisms were clearly created. They are far more complex that cars, and no one would claim the car evolved by natural selection. My notes and commentary on this work represent a very small portion of ideas from the book, and are put forth in my own words.

Also check out Behe's video course on Intelligent Design & Evolution: Course | Michael J. Behe (michaelbehe.com)

Note - the author starts off the book saying that he's ready to accept a very old Earth. This of course is a critical flaw in his analysis, but there is some diversity of opinion among the research that clearly establishes the flaws of evolutionary theory.

Ch.'s 1-2 The Box is Opened

Darwin could not see microbiology; he knew that the eye was for seeing, but he did not know how it saw; he did not have answers to these questions. **The cell is Darwin's Black box.** He had no clue how it worked.

Here is a brilliant analogy of what evolutionists claim with their millions of years of evolution from a common ancestor, of which there is no evidence. If your friend says he jumped over a couple of feet you believe him. If he says he jumped across 10 or 15 ft you are skeptical and surprised. If he says he jumped across the Grand Canyon, you don't believe him. Then he claims that it took him years to do it, and that there were buttes which he stood on in the canyon, which took a long time to appear, and which went away quickly after he had jumped. It's absurd. **Someone who claims that they made many small jumps to get across a large chasm in the past but that the things that jumped on are no longer there is very hard to believe.** *(Note - truly evolution is a system of belief, aka faith.)* Evolution makes huge leaps for which there is no evidence. There are **unbridgeable chasms even at the smallest levels of life**.

Darwin had to convince people that complex organisms could be made slowly.

Vision was a black box for Darwin. He and his contemporaries had no clue how it worked. What he thought was simple is extremely complex, involving many proteins enzymes etc.; multiple systems going at once.

99

These aren't just leap to leap, these are huge distances.

Darwinism explains micro evolution well (like the change in a bird's beak length over generations), but it is a farce to use this to explain the origins of life, the origins of species (like humans coming from sponges), the main thing that Darwin was getting at.

Little kids think a box can be an airplane (think Calvin & Hobbes) because they don't know how the airplane works. There are scientists now taking a similar approach about evolution and the origin of life!

Scientists used to think that cultures growing in a liquid could spontaneously generate because the flies appeared to spontaneously appear on meat. The key problem was to think that the flies and the cultures were extremely simple. A similar problem exists with the evolution of complex organs like the human eye. Darwin made it seem very simple, but it is not.

Neo-Darwinism was made by various sciences getting together and deciding what to do with evolution theory. This all came out before biochemistry. Now that we have biochemistry Neo-Darwinism must be revisited as biochemistry debunks it.

Darwinism is becoming less popular within and without of the scientific community due to many questions the theory cannot answer. Scientists admit that the theoretical framework and evidence for Neo-Darwinism is weak.

There appears to have been a biological 'Big Bang,' many species coming on scene at once.

Note: the "Cambrian Explosion" in the fossil record of advanced lifeforms appearing is from the flood of Noah wiping out many animals and fossilizing them in a unique environment able to convert bone into rock, something that isn't happening today.

Mathematicians insist that even with current dates of how old the Earth might be, that's not nearly enough time for claimed evolutionary changes in species.

Evolutionists are upset that
1. There are no transitional forms and
2. That species have different but very definite limits as to how much they can change and
3. That systems appear suddenly and
4. That natural selection cannot account for the diversity of life etc.

There have always been well-informed respected scientists who find Darwinism to be inadequate.

Most scientists will say they believe Darwinism, but they believe it based on authority, based on what others have said.

Scientists are afraid to debate natural selection, which fear is ironically unscientific. True science doesn't fear scrutiny challenge and debate.

When Richard Dawkins (arch evolutionist) tries to support the evolutionist view of the bombardier beetle evolving, he fails to explain how all those chambers, muscles, etc. would have evolved gradually. Many of the parts aren't necessary for the system and wouldn't have just shown up by and by. Even if you come up with a story of what might be beneficial here and there and how it might evolve, it still fails to explain the details of the extremely complex processes that would need to take place for such a story to come about. All they can say is that it might happen. That's not very scientific.

Richard Dawkins talks about the eye and explains it as a series of complex systems coming together. He never explains how those complex systems came to be in the first place. It's like saying a stereo is made from putting together an amplifier and a CD reader etc. without explaining how those parts first came to be and how they were assembled. Evolutionists use dramatic oversimplification to make it seem more plausible for something to have happened by chance.

These explanations given by Dawkins are extremely simple and do not justly describe how these things came to be. They are illogical assumptions that everything would be just right by chance. *(Note – it's all conjecture and supposition.)*

There are "irreducibly complex" systems which have no use until everything is in place. Natural selection can only choose systems that are already working.

You can make the case that multiple complex systems evolved at the same time just in time for a complex organism who needs all those multiple systems to live, but this is an empty argument; you might as well argue that the Earth popped into existence yesterday by chance.

LOOKING FOR APES IN MY FAMILY TREE

NOT SEEING IT

Evolutionists submit that evolution isn't always gradual, but they say it has to be gradual when explaining complex apparently designed objects like eyes because without gradual, all you have is miracle. You can't have it both ways!

A mutation can change one step of instruction such as 'place the legs on the head rather than on the abdomen,' but a mutation can't change the entire instructions such as 'instead of build a fax machine, build a radio.'

There are tens of thousands of different molecules involved with things like the eye and the bombardier beetle; you can't say that you know those all just evolved and came together. It is speculation, it is belief.

To debate about whether such evolution could randomly occur is like 19th century scientists debating about butterflies being able to spontaneously generate out of meat. Again, we simplify too much. And as we see the increasing complexity of these systems, the idea of random evolution to create them becomes less and less likely.

A mousetrap is an example of an irreducibly complex system; without all the parts there it doesn't catch any mice. Not only do you need to have all parts present at once, but all the parts need to be fine-tuned with just the right amount of spring, just the right positions, etc. An irreducibly complex system is assembled all at once.

Just because a bike is a precursor to a motorcycle doesn't mean the bike turned into the motorcycle. Biological evolution is limited to slight modifications and there's nothing about a bike that you can slightly modify into an engine or fuel tank. Natural selection in a bicycle manufacturing plant cannot produce a motorcycle. There is no example in history of major biological changes.

Note- there is the supposed Cambrian explosion but that is merely the fact that many fossils appeared seemingly out of nowhere; it's certainly not step by step proof of evolution. The reality of the Cambrian explosion (or other mass extinction claims) was the flood of Noah which brought about special conditions to fossilize many animals which in other conditions would have simply decayed.

In order to understand the barriers to evolution you must understand the complexity of biological systems.

Part 2 – Examining the Contents of the Box (Ch. 3-7)

\(This is where the complicated stuff is, and I won't attempt to give many notes here.)

Ch. 3 Flagella

Cells are run by molecular machines.

We make machines which efficiently do tasks, but in biology, if there is a microscopic machine doing a simple task efficiently, if that had to evolve, it would have had to learn that task too.

What something is made of and how it works are two different things, which are both extremely complex.

Evolutionists have very creative minds, they can come up with stories to explain evolution of anything, but they're just stories!

While modification goes on, systems are non-working.

The evolutionary literature explaining how these complex things would come to be is severely lacking. Further, the papers disagree with each other on the roads that would be taken, etc. They don't take into account mechanical details; they just make big generalizations.

Nobody knows how the flagella evolved. No research accounts for it etc. Some 40 different proteins are involved. It's the same for the cilia wherein some 200 different proteins are involved.

Cartoons show extremely complex systems going through a series of events to set off a single trap, it's humorous because everything must work exactly right to get the trap to go off - if one part of the whole sequence didn't work, the trap would fail. This is like evolution and it's laughable.

In biology there really are very complex systems which have an end function which is very specific, and it cannot be accounted for by evolution.

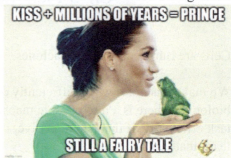

Note- it's like the old Paley's pocket watch in the desert analogy. If you find a pocket watch in the middle of the desert, do you conclude that it was put there by someone who owned purchased or created it, or do you conclude that it evolved randomly?

Ch. 4 Blood

Blood clotting is a very complex system of many interconnected parts. It has to form only when and where it is required or the whole system clots and dies. No one on earth has any idea how the coagulation current came to be.

Ch. 5-7 From Here to There; A Dangerous World; Roadkill

Each tiny little step in evolution has such small odds that it's utterly ridiculous to consider it. It's not just a small chance that one thing would evolve into another thing, it's a small chance that a very small part of the evolution would happen. And when we talk small, we mean infinitely small odds, making this more of a fairy tale storybook than science.

Natural selection only works if there's something useful already there to select from. Necessary proteins wouldn't just appear with nothing to do until other stuff arrived.

If one thing goes wrong in a whole delivery the package will not reach its destination and it may as well have never been sent.

Extremely complex processes take place billions of times a day in the cells of our bodies. Science is stranger than fiction. It cannot be accounted for by random evolution no matter how much time you give.

Note- Whenever we prove Darwin's macroevolution theory wrong, they just expand the age to an older and older Earth and universe. They can only play this game for so long; Darwinism is truly on its way out.

We see many irreducibly complex systems working together in even bigger irreducibly complex systems, and the mathematicians have said repeatedly that the current

107

age allowed for the Earth and universe is not nearly enough for these things to happen randomly; they would need to be at least billions and billions and billions and billions and billions and billions times billions and billions and billions and billions and billions of years older to give the remote chance. But as we can see this is nonsense, **you can't just sit around and take seriously a theory that requires so small odds**. The smacking obvious answer is that the Earth and universe were designed by a designer! You just can't get around that.

Irreducibly complex systems are all or nothing, you can't just add one part now and later add another part, or the system doesn't work.

You can't say that some parts of the cell were used for other functions before they were used in their current functions. It would leave a very lousy cell that would not sustain life. A single flaw in the cell's process pathway and you die. If cells evolved as incomplete structures our ancestors would have died too.

There's no literature on the evolution of vesicles and many other topics in the evolution of microbiology.

Part 3 What Does the Box Tell Us (Ch. 8-11)

Ch. 8-10 Publish or Perish; Intelligent Design; Questions about Design

The chemical soup life experiments failed miserably. Much guidance was given, and no complete life was made, etc.

There isn't a single book or article in scientific literature explaining the microbiological evolution. There are books and papers which say sequences but none of them say how those sequences came to be.

With a combination lock, if you keep trying different combinations, perhaps you eventually get half the letters right; this is not progress, you still can't open the lock, life can't reproduce to the next generation the "lock" fails. If the code is "Mary had a little lamb," the random choices with lots of time would just as soon spell out "Let's go to the park" or some other random sentence; the direction of the evolution wouldn't be aimed at or kept. No one is there to say which letters should be held to produce the correct sentence.

Some say that if there is a Designer why isn't nature more perfectly designed, but this is not the point of science. The point of science is to see whether design is obvious. We cannot guess the psychology of the designer as to why certain systems would be imperfect.

Note- of course sin results in damaged systems - ever since the fall of Adam our bodies have been fallen and broken, tending toward decay and death; and when this life is viewed as a probation/test to see how we respond to weakness, it is better understood why systems are intentionally imperfect.

Vestigial organs which have no apparent use are claimed to be by-products of trial-and-error evolution from past species, however these supposedly useless organs turn out to be extremely important in immunity etc. Just because we don't know why something is there doesn't mean it's useless.

Once design is taken seriously by scientists, academic literature will be much more rigorous, require much more hard data, and **tolerate much less storytelling**.

The author says there's a possibility of old earth with intelligent design.

Note- True, but I don't see a need for it, old earth was specifically theorized to get rid of a creator and add time for random/natural mutation. Evidence is piling up against old earth theory.

Ch. 11 Science Philosophy and Religion

The discovery that life was made by intelligent design is one of the single greatest discoveries of all science.

About 90% of Americans believe in God and about half attend religious services regularly. The army employs chaplains. Businesses and sport teams gather for prayers. As a country we honor people like Martin Luther King whose actions were deeply rooted in a belief in God.

The 1925 John Scopes trial involved Scopes, a teacher who volunteered to be arrested for a law to not teach about the Creator in science. There's a movie about it called "Inherit the Wind" (1960).

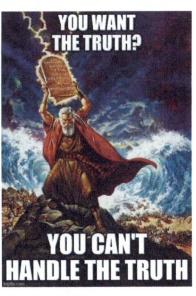

Note- Inherit the Wind makes the preachers and creationists look like idiots, and the evolutionists to be the only ones with level heads and sense. The creationists don't even try to use any scientific evidence, so the evolutionists simply take the side of "science," and claim that the religious are in the way of all science. They think all evolutionists must do to refute creationism is to simply poke at supposed errors of the Bible. That Darwinism is scientifically impossible was completely avoided.

One man who performed many science experiments was going to be hired but was asked in the interview if he believed in evolution. He said no, he believed in the biblical account of creation, and for this he was not hired.

Science these days is less of a pursuit for truth and more of a game played by the rule that the supernatural can never be invoked. Professional scientists in university accept this rule even when they privately believe in God, as most of the population does.

A Designer can't be put in a test tube but neither can extinct (supposed and missing) common ancestors. We can see the lingering effects of a designer (just like how they claim to see lingering effects of the missing common ancestor).

Note – it seems the missing common ancestor is their god. All hail the invisible sponge king!

Scientists try to place the origin of all life in the universe in a tiny box, but it cannot be done.

Evolutionists want to force parents to teach children evolution.

Note- one way they are accomplishing this is by putting more and more restrictions on homeschooling. Use this freedom while you still have it. Fear God, not man.

The fear that science with supernatural conclusions would ruin science is not founded.

It is not a strange conclusion that life was designed by an intelligent agent; rather that is the obvious and natural conclusion.

Afterward

Over the past decade since the book this book was originally published we have learned much more about microbiology, how things are even more complex, and this strengthens the case of intelligent design.

Some say that these irreducibly complex systems could be used for other things as they break into simpler machines, but this is devolution not evolution.

The author never said that parts of the irreducibly complex system couldn't be used for something else. He said the removal of one part causes the whole system to stop functioning; it doesn't necessarily cause the individual parts to stop functioning.

Mouse traps weren't made by a handful of toothpicks getting together and deciding to be a mousetrap.
You might as well assume that half of your car's transmission will jump out of your airbag. Essential components don't happily come out of accessories.

Richard Dawkins said biology is the study of living things that *appear* to have been designed. Thus we see that **even to the diehard Darwinists design is evident. It's not just some conclusion we draw when we can't think of anything else.** It's what we conclude when we get in touch with our inner ingenuity. Any engineer can pick out something that's been designed for a purpose and he can usually pick out the purpose by looking at the structure of the objects.
The difficult thing would be to make the claim that random evolution is responsible for these things.
The burden of proof is on the one who denies what he can plainly see with his eyes. In the absence of an explanation, we are rationally justified to assume complex things like

Mount Rushmore were designed, not just evolved.

"All sciences begin with speculation, only Darwinism ends with it." Authors promoting evolution acknowledge this, that their work is speculation.

Assertions that microscopic machines evolved are based in speculation, not calculations and experiments.

There are no detailed Darwinian accounts for the evolution of anything.

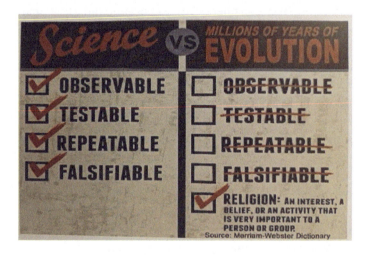

Darwin on Trial by Phillip E. Johnson - Book Highlights & Commentary

Ch. 1- 4

The 1960 movie 'Inherit the Wind' made fun of creation science advocates, mocking people who didn't want evolution taught because of its atheistic themes. But what wasn't pointed out is that the person advocating evolution also advocated several bogus Neanderthal finds like 'Nebraska Man' who was like the tooth of a pig, which was said to be the tooth of a hominid monkey-man. The evolutionist argued using many falsehoods.

Just because we don't have the whole answer to replace evolution doesn't mean we can't point out how wrong evolution is.

Survival of the fittest is just a tautology saying that those who leave the most offspring leave the most offspring. It doesn't tell us anything.

Different types of eyes in the animal kingdom are not just examples of increasing complexity. There are over 40 different types of eyes. And 5% of an eye is not the same as 5% vision; only the complete eye gives any vision at all, and only with the proper receptor.

A program designed to scramble a book would not turn the book into a different language and it would not turn the book into a book on a different topic.

Opponents of Darwin were leading geologists and paleontologists; it wasn't just religious objection.

Opponents of Darwin such as George Cuvier were fossil experts who saw no gradual change but rather saw signs of various Extinctions and creations of new species.

Note - I do not see a necessity for the theory of multiple mass extinctions and multiple creations, it can all be easily accounted for in the catastrophic flood. Either way, the data doesn't support evolution.

Darwin said nature must have hidden the transitional forms!

Lots more study of the fossil record has been done since Darwin. Darwin relied on the claim that we haven't looked enough for transitional fossils, but today we know that new kinds of animals don't appear gradually, but suddenly.

Note - and by 'new' it could just mean different, as in placed down at a different level instead of a second creation. Fossils represent death. Again, either way, the key is that we don't see gradual forms, as evolution requires.

No intermediates are found in the fossil record. Evolutionists try to explain away the sudden changes in the fossil record without transitional fossils by saying that the new fossil must have evolved over a fast geological period of time, as in hundreds of thousands of years. They say, 'because Earth is so old we have all this time to work with.'

The Cambrian explosion is a major problem for evolutionists - nearly all the animals appear there without predecessors.

Note – some say the flood is a different extinction such as the Permian/Triassic with the Cambrian being the fall of Adam, but most the evidence I've seen points to the Cambrian as the flood. I have low confidence in claims of multiple mass extinctions, though there certainly have been multiple catastrophic events in human history.

Based on modern fossilization theory we should not have any soft tissues which fossilized yet we do have them.

Note - the flood created the perfect setting for fossilization, making the fossil record one big testament of divine power and intervention.

Evolution calls for species to die out slowly and gradually. But this is not what we see, we see mass extinction. The record does not show gradual development; scientists are aware of this.

Stasis, a lack of change, is the norm in the fossil record. Evolutionists came up with punctuated equilibrium theory to try and explain the lack of transitional fossils by claiming there were semi-fast changes (within hundreds of thousands) which have not left behind fossil evidence. So here we have invisible evidence of evolution, awesome!

Scientists know that fossils don't work well for evolution, they are embarrassed of this and they're under tremendous pressure when publishing about fossils to somehow make them fit with evolution theory.

Note – I remember in one debate an evolutionist kept trying to get away from fossils. He said, 'we don't even need fossils anymore!' as he attempted to change the conversation to genetics, which of course has its own plethora of obvious problems for evolution. I'm also reminded of the famous evolutionary plant biologist who, when asked what the best evidence for evolution was, said, 'the whale pelvis!' Apparently, nothing in his own field of study was compelling, and he had to turn to vague optimistic claims from another field. Of course, the whale pelvis is needed for reproduction and isn't vestigial at all.

Ch. 5 The 'Fact' of Evolution

Evolutionists use descent with modification to explain difficulties in classification.

118

Evolutionists insist that no matter how much evidence you give against evolution, nothing makes sense except for evolution.

Fossils do not show links between different species in the phylogenic tree.

Labs are unable to show the process of change from one species into another.

Recasting the theory as fact serves no purpose other than to protect it from falsification.

Darwinists point to microevolution and claim that such is evidence for major change between species though we have no mechanism for macroevolution (species change). It's never been shown and no fossil evidence for it exists.

Note – you can't say 'well we haven't waited millions of years, so you don't know that macroevolution doesn't happen.' For one this is shifting the burden of proof, and for two a vague claim that something might happen in millions of years is inherently untestable and therefore inherently unscientific. Evolution should be classed with philosophy or religion, not science. Evolution wouldn't last long anywhere without tax funding and monopolistic control on other disciplines.

Google says there are three reasons why evolution is a fact.
1. **Microevolution**.

Note - Here they apply one process to something it has nothing to do with, like saying because I can jump on a pogo stick, that I should also be able to jump to the moon.

2. **Nature is imperfect** so it must not have been done by intelligence.

Note – here they assume the motives of the Creator. How do they know He isn't building in weakness into the system for a reason? Further, pointing out imperfections doesn't account for all the mind-boggling order in nature, allowing for life.

3. **Hominids** and mammals which are like reptiles.

Note – these claims are based on conjecture and minor differences in skeletons which are easily accounted for in variation of known species, etc.

Ch. 6 Invertebrate Sequence

Evolution says we've got to have animalistic ancestors, so we'll pick these ones because they're the best candidates. They are looking for ways to support their theory rather than questioning the theory (and comparing the theory to all the evidence nature provides).

Evolution theory said ancestors must be there, so they insist that something they find is in fact those ancestors.

There are claims about transitional fossils between amphibians and fish, but these are wild speculations. No explanation exists about how an amphibian could have developed reptilian reproduction based on Darwinian descent. The difference between a fossil mammal and a fossil reptile is very slim based on just a few jawbones and often it can go either way.

Note – only basing classification on bones is a fallacy often adopted by evolutionists. They would tell you that my arm and my dog's arm are neigh indistinguishable!

If all mammals descended from a common animal the fossil record would show the transition, but it does not. So, evolutionists have put forth a theory of mammals having descended from multiple different preliminary creatures instead of one like Darwin said.

Note – arguments like this get shut down quickly, Darwinism falls apart when you start allowing multiple ancestors. In truth, God created many types of animals for this world.

The Archeopteryx fossil is a bird with teeth and claws which they claim as a transitional fossil between reptiles and birds. This is not necessarily evidence of a reptile becoming a bird, it may be like the modern platypus which has some features of one animal type and other features of another. Evolutionists do not know what necessary processes would have occurred to change from a reptiles scales into birds feathers and bird's lungs, etc.

Note – there are also other birds which have teeth and claws. And more typical birds have been found in 'lower' geologic layers than Archeopteryx, leaving scientists to admit that they must look for the transitional fossil elsewhere.

Google originally published about 12 hominid species establishing the link between humans and monkeys later had had to reduce it to five.

Note – they like to claim all sorts of finds, but it's the same story of hoaxes and imaginative supposition.

The theory of evolution was accepted first, and later they came up with their supporting evidence for it of transitional humans. With their theory in hand evolutionists went hunting everywhere for the evidence to support it. The theory did not come from a bunch of transitional skeletons we didn't know what to do with, these transitional skeletons were **invented to support the pre-existing idea** that we needed them!

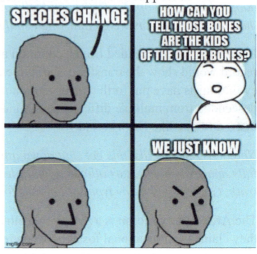

Public pressure to find the missing link between humans and monkeys was so great that there were lots of frauds. Piltdown man was one of these frauds that lasted for 40 years before it was detected because they kept it heavily guarded. We see what we expect to see unless we are extremely rigorous in checking our prejudice. Nebraska man was another known fraud.

Note – there are two types of hominids. Known frauds, and undetected frauds.

Many scientists doubt that there's much difference in the limited species between monkeys and humans and suggest these are actually the same species.

Genetic evidence of the mitochondrial eve shuts down a lot of hominid claims limiting them to a couple hundred thousand years.

Whales are very complex with lots of features which couldn't have evolved over time such as their ability to swim deep and their ability to use sonar and their ability for the young to suckle without taking in water. Even the vestigial legs are a problem of great complexity which evolution has no answers for such as when and how they would have come.

Darwin conceded that fossil evidence weighs heavily against his theory and the same holds true today. This is why they avoid talking about fossils and try to focus on molecular evidence.

Ch. 7 The Molecular Evidence

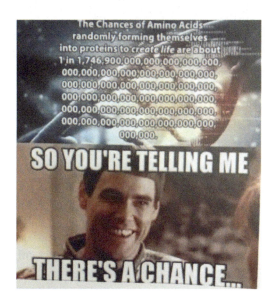

Darwinists conveniently claim that all the transitional species **quickly died so we don't have evidence** of them existing.

Evolutionists do not insist that natural selection is the only method for speciation, but they are very vague about what else could have happened.

There are no transitional species between single cellular and multicellular life.

No explanation is given for the difference between apes and humans; no explanation for why they're different or how they became different. *(Note – no legitimate cohesive reasonable sufficiently-detailed explanation, at least.)*

There's no empirical evidence that transitional species link together any distance distance to a single ancestor, and no evidence this common ancestor existed.

If molecular change occurred, it must have been at clock-like intervals, not depending on environmental changes as evolution suggests.

Change ACROSS species (speculative)

Change WITHIN species (demonstratable)

Just because two molecular forms are different does not imply natural selection.

There's no evidence that natural selection has creative power. (Note – nature selects, it doesn't create new material to select from. It can show survival of the fittest, but not arrival of the fittest. Further, beneficial mutations are extremely rare and short-lived.)

Many scientists advocate that the molecular clock says humans evolved from a common ancestor in Africa less than 200,000 years ago. Many evolutionists don't like this because it rules out a lot of the hominid transitional species from an older time and other location.

We can't just look at molecular evolution because the molecules had to be housed in organisms which would have had to evolve along with the molecules.

The real mystery is how a simple thing could have turned into a complex thing.

Molecular information adds to the complexity showing that these are complex machinery requiring the cooperation of multiple parts to carry out their function.

Note – every field of science brings more complexity to the table and makes evolution that much more ridiculous.

The hemoglobin is so complex it's called the molecular lung.

The more complex molecular biology is the less likely there could have been mechanisms to transform one kind into another and time to do it.

Note – this is why evolutionists are in the business of downplaying complexity, and lengthening timeframes.

Testing Darwinism by molecular evidence is never even attempted.

Ch. 8 Pre-biological Evolution

Pre-biological evolution refers to chemicals and how chemicals evolved.

When the Supreme Court **struck down** Louisiana's law that you must teach creation science in addition to evolution science, chief justice Scalia dissented because he knew that the people of Louisiana deserve to teach evidence which doesn't support evolution. (Note – Scalia wanted more academic freedom, less of a monopoly on science. He wanted science to point out the pros and cons of multiple theories. Too bad Scalia was the minority losing voice!)

When scientists use the word evolution, they're trying to say an explanation of everything from the Big Bang to the present without allowing any role for a creator (intelligent designer).

Note - evolution is multi-disciplinary, a spreading malicious cancer killing all truth.

The Miller Yuri experiment was about taking several amino acids and attempting to spark them into a protein, but this is flawed for multiple reasons, one of which is they already started out with the amino acids.

An organism forming from prebiotic soup is about as unlikely as a tornado going through a junkyard making an airplane. These microorganisms are more complex than a spaceship, yet we say they assembled by chance? No matter how much time you give, this is bizarre.

The prokaryotic bacterial cell is much more complex than a spaceship.

'Chance assembly' is another way of saying miracle.

Materialists (who dominate modern science) insist that there cannot be any supernatural element in the creation of life.

Note – and no purpose allowed either. Jonathan Wells talks about the Smithsonian refusing to air a program on evolution which also suggested there may be some purpose in life. The evolutionists wildly protested the presentation and got it canceled. Nothing but complete atheistic secular humanism satisfies them. They must dominate all scientific discussion and ban any who violate their arbitrary definitions of what is and isn't 'science.'

If life were so easy to make it would have happened many times in many places.

A popular theory is that the first RNA managed to synthesize itself from prebiotic soup, without proteins. Though this is conceivable it is not probable or experimentally verifiable. There are many creative theories about how the first life may have come into being, but none of them are experimentally verifiable.

Note – as Isaac Newton said, "A man may imagine things that are false, but he can only understand things that are true."

All theories are acceptable so long as none of them are creationism, in other words an intelligent agent creating something; they don't allow God to be involved in creation at any level or in any way.

Note – what if God is actually how the creation happened? What if all the evidence points to God? Now you can see how unscientific we become as we insist on these arbitrary parameters, and exclude the Truth (God) which nature points to.

Crick (one of the discoverers of DNA) and others recognize the extreme difficulty of creating life on Earth, especially within the parameters of time allotted, even though the time allotted is very long. These skeptical scientists speculate that life arrived here from some other place in space, microscopic life on an asteroid or something. That would mean this life would have to travel through space safely and remain alive.

Crick says there may have been an extra-terrestrial civilization who sent bacteria into space to start life on another planet. (Note – as I recall even Richard Dawkins accepts this possibility; he says alien life forms could have placed early life here. These ideas are much closer to the truth than cosmic and chemical evolution.)

Critics of the extra-terrestrial implant theory have issue with the invisibility of these extraterrestrials, but we also are working with invisible transitional hominid species.

When you must invoke invisible spacemen, it's time to admit that your theory of evolution doesn't work.

Ch. 9 The Rules of Science

Evolution has become **orthodox,** and no one dares stray from it. The fight in Louisiana to allow creation science to be taught in school, or rather to require it to be taught if evolution is taught, was struck down by people trying to uphold the orthodoxy of evolution and liberal religion, afraid of religious fanatics.

Note – ironically, their censorship of non-evolution friendly ideas has made them the new fanatics. (This concept of orthodoxy was from earlier in the book.)

They define science by whatever is accepted by the scientific community, meaning the official scientific community.

Science is supposed to be guided by natural law and testable with tentative conclusions which are falsifiable. They say creation science doesn't fit the criteria because it's not falsifiable or testable as it points to supernatural creation. But scientists study gravity, and they can't explain gravity by natural law.

Note – just as gravity is a law which we observe yet don't fully understand, why not roll out the law of design? The law of creation? Sure, we don't understand it yet, but let's put a name to what we all are seeing rather than trying to pin it on something we aren't seeing.

Mainstream science says young Earth and the flood are false, but how can they say that if this science is unfalsifiable?

Creationists argue that Earth and life had to be designed regardless of how long it took or what way it was done. Then

130

evolution has to answer why it's against the possibility that nature was designed. Evolutionists advocate naturalistic developments without purpose, no conscious purpose or direction. *(Note – it's a tall order defending that position!)*

The scientific community is clear in their advocacy that God was in no way involved in evolution.

Note – evolution is all about a theory of nature making itself. That's the whole point. Why Christians turn to this vomit for substantive truth is beyond me.

Naturalist scientists only believe in God when God is an abstract concept, uninvolved in nature.

Note – a perfect fit for the Devil's kingdom. Incomprehensible & useless. Those acquainted with the teachings of the restored gospel should be the first to object.

131

Scientific naturalism is espoused by the theory of evolution. Evolution requires naturalism and it says whatever can't be seen (detected by common methods) isn't real. Evolution uses (empirical) naturalism as the only way of finding truth.

Naturalism says all of nature is a closed system of cause and effects not influenced by anything outside.

Naturalism denies that a supernatural being could influence natural events such as evolution, or communicate with natural creatures such as ourselves.

Note – Evolution doesn't work even with the 'God used evolution' claim, and for many reasons. Evolution is a wasteful cruel process of trial and error. Evolution doesn't have God's signature in any way. There are so many better ways that God could have created. We must remember that removing God from the picture is the only reason evolutionary theory was designed in the first place.

The absence of a Creator is the <u>essential</u> starting point for Darwinism.

Empiricists are willing to dismiss any doctrine that doesn't match with their limited scientific evidence.

Darwinism is not empirical! You can't observe creation by natural selection any more than you can observe creation by God. Natural selection exists but it's going really far out to say it has such creative power. The fossil record does not match the gradual changes that Darwinism implies. When it comes to explaining the origins of life and species, Darwinism is pure philosophy. If empiricism was the top goal, Darwinism would have been limited to observable microevolution with no important philosophical or theological implications.

They've typed up a bunch of rules about what science is that keep anyone from doing anything which isn't naturalistic, and they've declared that everything which is science is truth and everything which is not science is false.

In making these arbitrary rules scientists **dismiss entire arguments from the onset and simply claim that advocates of these dissenting ideas don't understand** how science works.

Note – modern science has become a good old boys club rather than an evidence-based institution.

In one moment, evolutionists say they don't deal with religion. In the next they make sweeping statements about the purpose of the cosmos.

When a **paradigm** is established, it serves as **a grand organizing principle.** The paradigm of evolution has become the **lens through which we view everything** and the way we study everything.

The problem of stasis in the fossil record was not described for a very long time because **Darwinists did not want to put it to print**. This is an example of how a certain paradigm can limit our understanding of nature.

Naturalistic evolutionists don't bother with whether something is true or not, they only say it's the best way of describing things and may change in the future.

Note - in other words they deny our ability to discover laws of nature or that such even exist. They no longer are engaged in the pursuit of truth.

Since science (particularly evolutionary science) has the **monopoly on knowledge, that now has to explain philosophical and theological** questions.

They insist that this is not just their way of seeing things, it's the only way, and they're trying to convert everyone to it.

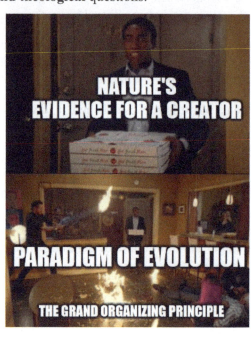

Note – long have the creationists made the modest request that both sides be taught.
Evolutionists can't stand this idea.

Ch. 10 Darwinist Religion

Modern science claims that anything which can't be proven (particularly proven their way) is a mere superstition, a feeling. (*Note – an outdated crutch people are growing out of.*)

It is said that those who accept religion and science have to check (leave) their brains at the church door.

Note – must we check our faith at the school door? Neither option is acceptable.

Modern science is at war with creationism and **demands absolute surrender.**

An organization called ASA of Christian scientists wanted to claim that you can have it both ways with evolution and the Bible, and the science establishment came down hard on them for allowing any sort of God to be involved in any way, demanding that such involvement is unscientific.

The message of secular humanism advocated by John Dewey etc. is that **salvation is by science**. They see science as the answer to everything.

Secular philosophers praise evolution's ability to control the destiny of mankind.

Evolution isn't just a theory, it's a theory to which all other theories must bow. It is the light that illuminates all, is the god we must worship, it is taking us to heaven.

Note - The Book of Mormon describes the great abominable church of the devil as having dominion over all the Earth, and this does seem to fit the bill, particularly in light of its takeover of all other sciences, its self-declared tyranny over all methods of learning, and its forceful attempts to be the only voice allowed to answer questions of philosophy & theology.

Evolution is indoctrination, not education.

Ch. 11 Darwinist Education

Darwinism is deduced by logic, not experimental evidence.

Scientific theories are often related to social theories.

HOW DO YOU EXPLAIN YOUR HORRIFIC ACT OF VIOLENCE?

I IDENTIFY AS A HOMINID ANIMAL WHOSE MORALS HAVE NOT YET EMERGED

One exhibit said that Darwinism is one of several theories about the origin of Life etc. The evolutionists promptly got this taken down and replaced it with a sign that said the evidence supports Darwinism.

Policies avoid referring to evolution itself, rather they refer to 'science,' not wanting to admit that evolution is a special case of controversy.

Teachers and students are not allowed to discuss disbelief in Darwinism any more than they're allowed to discuss disbelief in 2 + 2 = 4.

Note - education is supposed to be non-dogmatic and evidence based, to promote understanding. Evolution dogmatically taught in school is about gaining converts to an orthodox theory.

They say evolution belongs to the category of knowledge not belief, yet we must **believe** in these transitional fossils we can't see, **believe** in life sparking into existence on its own, and **believe** in one species transforming into another, which is never been observed.

The language that evolution is couched in is calculated more to conceal knowledge than to portray it.

Ch. 12 Science & Pseudoscience

Marx made predictions and when those predictions failed to come to pass, his followers modified his predictions, so it looked like they still came to pass.

Note - surely Marx is the anti-prophet of the apocalypse, born shortly after the true prophet Joseph Smith.

People base their entire careers on theories like evolution and they're afraid to see them go down.

Freud was a pseudoscientist. *(Note - A 'fraud')*

The word evolution means lots of different things. The trick is to use it to prove something very simple and then apply that to everything else. Demonstrate a minor change and use that to claim that major changes happen.

Amongst themselves Darwinists blame everything on natural selection. When criticized about just how that works, they change the subject to molecular evolution and claim that we don't even really need natural selection because there are other methods.

When molecular science came around it was just what the evolutionist had predicted… just after they changed the theory of evolution to accommodate the new information.

Evolutionists call anyone who believes in an involved creator who is involved a 'religious fundamentalist.'

Scientists are devoted to **protecting** evolution, not defending it.

Scientific naturalism is philosophical, not scientific.

Additional Resources

See Gary Shapiro's blog "No Death Before the Fall" at
http://ndbf.blogspot.com.

Book "Man: His Origin and Destiny" by Joseph Fielding
Smith. This is both a great dissertation on Church doctrines,
and has several chapters specifically refuting claims of
evolutionary theory, including pointing out the errors in
evolutionary science. This book was written by an Apostle
and was advocated by the Church for many years. Members
of the Quorum of the 12 urged him to write it, and President
Benson highly recommended it. Get a copy and see for
yourself! https://www.amazon.com/Origin-Destiny-Joseph-
Fielding-Smith/dp/B00073363I

Book "Universal Model: A New Millennial Science." (2
volumes) (UniversalModel.com) This is a terrific academic
resource put together by a member of the Church which
demonstrates the geologic fact of Noah's worldwide flood, a
young earth, the impossibility of evolution from monkeys,
and so on.

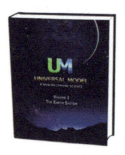

Book "Using the Book of Mormon to Combat Falsehoods in Organic Evolution" by Clark Peterson.

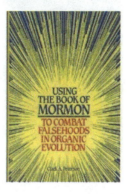

Dissent from Darwin: Scientists unite in expressing doubt in claims of Darwin's theory: https://dissentfromdarwin.org

Book "Science and Religion: Reconciling the Conflicts" by David Barker. This book by a latter-day saint researcher does a good job showing that the science which doesn't match the Bible is actually not good science, such as the flawed dating methods.
Purchase it here: https://a.co/d/5oNfz1u

Book "The Evolution Cruncher." Get a free PDF of this excellent book and succeeding editions here
https://evolutionfacts.com/Downloads.htm

Book "In The Beginning by Walt Brown." Get a free PDF of this excellent book here
https://creationism.org/books/index.htm

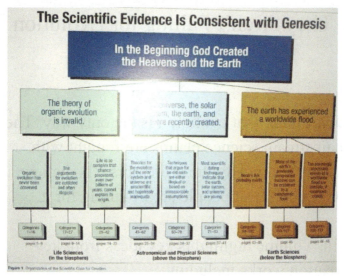

Figure 1: Organization of the Scientific Case for Creation.

A great resource to begin creation science study with many free resources is creationism.org, where you can access the Kent Hovind lecture slides & many creation flagship books as free PDFs.

Jeremy Michel's Dinosaurs in Scripture presentation: Dinosaurs in Scriptures, Dragons, Living Dinosaurs, and Noah's Flood. (youtube.com)

Book "Doctrinal Foundations of the Creation of Life" by Lee H. Pearson, PhD (An LDS View & Scientific Evidence).

Book "Bones of Contention." Refutes leading hominid bone claims in detail.

Book "From Darwin to Hitler: Evolutionary Ethics, Eugenics and Racism in Germany" by Richard Weikart.

They Aren't Falling for Evolution

And you don't have to either!

Don't think that evolution is the only way. The mainstream science claims are fraught with issues. It's mostly the professors who believe in evolution; most people aren't falling for it.

This volume highlights key ideas from key creation works including:

Universal Model: A New Millennial Science by Dean Sessions
Darwin's Doubt by Stephen Meyer
Scientific Creationism by Henry Morris
Darwin's Black Box by Michael Behe
The Politically Incorrect Guide to Darwinism by Jonathan Wells
Darwin on Trial by Phillip Johnson
Ark in the Darkness
Dragons or Dinosaurs
Is Genesis History
And more!

Made in the USA
Monee, IL
13 December 2024